(Extra)Ordinary?

At the Interface/Probing the Boundaries

Series Editor

Rob Fisher (*Oxford, United Kingdom*)

Advisory Board

Peter Bray (*University of Auckland, New Zealand*)
Robert Butler (*Elmhurst College, Illinois, USA*)
Ioana Cartarescu (*Bucharest, Romania*)
Seán Moran (*Waterford Institute of Technology, Ireland*)
Stephen Morris (*New York, USA*)
John Parry (*Lewis & Clark Law School, Portland, Oregon, USA*)
Natalia Kaloh Vid (*University of Maribor, Slovenia*)

VOLUME 101

The titles published in this series are listed at *brill.com/aipb*

(Extra)Ordinary?

The Concept of Authenticity in Celebrity and Fan Studies

Edited by

Jade Alexander
Katarzyna Bronk

BRILL
RODOPI

LEIDEN | BOSTON

Cover illustration: Yavdat (on fotolia.com). Used with permission.

The Library of Congress Cataloging-in-Publication Data is available online at http://catalog.loc.gov
LC record available at http://lccn.loc.gov/

Typeface for the Latin, Greek, and Cyrillic scripts: "Brill". See and download: brill.com/brill-typeface.

ISSN 1570-7113
ISBN 978-90-04-36658-9 (paperback)
ISBN 978-90-04-36695-4 (e-book)

Copyright 2018 by Koninklijke Brill NV, Leiden, The Netherlands.
Koninklijke Brill NV incorporates the imprints Brill, Brill Hes & De Graaf, Brill Nijhoff, Brill Rodopi, Brill Sense and Hotei Publishing.
All rights reserved. No part of this publication may be reproduced, translated, stored in a retrieval system, or transmitted in any form or by any means, electronic, mechanical, photocopying, recording or otherwise, without prior written permission from the publisher.
Authorization to photocopy items for internal or personal use is granted by Koninklijke Brill NV provided that the appropriate fees are paid directly to The Copyright Clearance Center, 222 Rosewood Drive, Suite 910, Danvers, MA 01923, USA. Fees are subject to change.

This book is printed on acid-free paper and produced in a sustainable manner.

Contents

Notes on Contributors VII

Introduction: (Extra)Ordinary? 1
    Jade Alexander and Katarzyna Bronk

PART 1
Constructing Celebrity

1. "The Big Fellow Is Dead!": Michael Collins as Celebrity and Nationalist Martyr 11
    Amber Anna Colvin

2. Mediating Bieber in Canada: Authenticating Nation in Fame 34
    Samita Nandy

3. Literary Celebrity, Politics and the Nobel Prize: The Nobel Lecture as an Authorial Self-Fashioning Platform 54
    Sandra Mayer

PART 2
(Re)Envisioning Stardom

4. Oscar Wilde's Long Afterlife: Victorian Celebrity and Its Transformations in Modern Culture 77
    Anna Fomichenko

5. Touching Fame: Exploring Interactional Dynamics between Local Celebrities and Fans in Sydney's Roller Derby Scene 93
    Jade Alexander

6. Celebrity Awards, Fan Communities and the Reconstruction of "High" and "Low" Cultures 119
    Mira Moshe

Index 137

Notes on Contributors

Jade Alexander
completed her PhD on roller derby culture at Western Sydney University, Australia. While she is interested in women's sport more broadly—having previously completed research on women's soccer—this study of roller derby explored celebrity and fandom, as well as gender, the body and injury, sport and performance, and community and sociality. She currently tutors in the School of Humanities and Communication Arts at Western Sydney University in cultural studies, sociology, and gender studies subjects.

Katarzyna Bronk
is Assistant Professor at the Faculty of English, Adam Mickiewicz University in Poznan, Poland. She teaches the History of English Literature, but specialises in English theatre and drama and, thus, investigated the question of celebrity within it. While researching questions of social hierarchy, ostracism as well as the ways of celebrating certain individuals, she turned her studies towards Humanist Gerontology as seen in theatre. In 2015 she was awarded a research grant from the Polish Ministry of Science and Higher Education to study old age and ageing in English theatre/drama between 1660 and 1750, and her first edited collection on this topic, *Autumnal Faces: Old Age in British and Irish Dramatic Narratives*, was published in 2017.

Amber Anna Colvin
is a doctoral student at the University of Memphis in Early Modern British History and the Coordinator of the Lausanne Learning Institute. She is currently finishing her dissertation on the connections and interactions between royal portraiture and conceptions of family in the reigns of Henry VIII, James II, and George II.

Anna Fomichenko
is a graduate of the Russian State University for the Humanities (RSUH), Moscow. Her research mainly focuses on the 19th-century English literature and celebrity culture. She is currently working as an independent scholar and teaching English as foreign language, as well as doing research in the ELT sphere.

Sandra Mayer
is a senior research and teaching associate in English Literature at the University of Zurich, Switzerland, and a Visiting Scholar at the Oxford Centre

for Life-Writing (OCLW), Wolfson College. She has just completed her monograph on the reception of Oscar Wilde on twentieth-century Viennese stages, and she is currently working on a book that explores the interrelations of literary celebrity and politics in and through autobiographical life-writing genres. Her co-edited journal special issues on the themes of "Life-Writing and Celebrity" for *Life Writing* and "The Author in the Popular Imagination" for *Forum for Modern Language Studies* are forthcoming in 2018.

Mira Moshe
is a senior lecturer at Ariel University, Israel. Her publications include: a co-edited book, *The Walk of Shame* (2013), *The Emotion Industry* (2014), and *Temporal Love: Temporality and Romantic Relationships* (2016), all published by Nova Science Publishers, Inc., New York, NY. In addition, Dr. Moshe has published the results of her work, which has mainly focused on the media, politics, culture and society, in leading academic journals and collections of articles.

Samita Nandy
holds a Doctorate from the School of Media, Culture and Creative Arts (MCCA) at Curtin University in Australia. Her work has been sponsored by international and national, federal and provincial, grants and awards in Australia and Canada. Nandy has expertise in postgraduate and honours teaching at University of Toronto, Ryerson University, and Curtin University. She is the Founder of the Centre for Media and Celebrity Studies (CMCS) and her research focuses on celebrities and cultural meanings of fame in a national context.

Introduction: (Extra)Ordinary?

Jade Alexander and Katarzyna Bronk

P. David Marshall sees celebrity not only as the "key trope" of our contemporary culture but also, perhaps more importantly, as "the lingua franca of identity" in modern times.[1] What this suggests is that, whether we want it or not, we measure our own value, as well as the value of our everyday life, against popular and celebrated individuals with which the media keep constantly bombarding us. The question to be additionally asked is who those celebrated individuals are in the twenty-first century.

If one takes the broadest definition of celebrity into consideration, then the points of reference, or relevance, have to be chosen among James Monaco's heroes, stars and "quasars,"[2] or among these whose celebrity has been "ascribed," "achieved" or "attributed," as termed by Chris Rojek.[3] This way, however, the potential group of role models—in terms of behaviour and/or lifestyle—or perhaps the objects of envy, becomes so numerous that, consequently, the choice seems to diminish in quality. After all, considering the above-mentioned categories, such a powerful group of influence would consist of the likes of, let us say, the Beatles, Oscar Wilde, President Obama, Lady Gaga, Justin Trudeau, David Beckham, the crew of MTV's *Jersey Shore*[4] and, to finish with the colloquial "bang," Pope Francis himself. While almost every member of this celebrity "sample" seems an obvious choice, the final candidate might come as a bit of a surprise, even though Chris Rojek has already proved that celebrity and religion are tightly intertwined.

If one sees contemporary celebrities as either fabricated, or produced, for intended consumption of the proverbial masses, and adds to this the "accidental (anti-)heroes" of the ever-popular reality shows who gain popularity through media exposure, then the Roman Catholic leader indeed seems out of place. However, it is Pope Francis who appeared on the January cover of *RollingStone*

---

[1] P. David Marshall, "Introduction," in *The Celebrity Culture Reader*, ed. P. David Marshall (New York: Routledge, 2006), 3.

[2] James Monaco as discussed in Graeme Turner, *Understanding Celebrity* (London: Sage, 2010), 21–2.

[3] Chris Rojek as discussed in Graeme Turner, *Understanding Celebrity* (London: Sage, 2010), 22. See also Chris Rojek, *Celebrity* (London: Reaktion Books, 2001).

[4] For more see MTV's series webpage.

magazine in 2014. "It's a funny thing, papal celebrity,"[5] states Mark Binelli in the feature on the 266th leader of the Holy See. The magazine cover, with the gently smiling new Pope, caused a bit of a stir among the faithful readership of the pop culture oriented publication. This iconic representation, however, comes as less of a surprize when one realises that the value of the Pontiff has already been recognised by other secular media. He also featured on the cover of *Time* magazine, all due to receiving the title of the 2013 "Person of the Year."[6]

Taking this sudden celebrity-like (media) popularity of the Pontiff into account, one should perhaps investigate the notions of "celebritydom" a bit further, and this is what the present volume wishes to engage in. The authors, whose chapters make up this inter-disciplinary volume, utilise the existing research on celebrity and fandom, but they also go beyond the often quoted theorists, and engage in multidirectional analyses of what it means to be a celebrity and what influence they have on the consuming public. The subsequent chapters engage in research on individuals representing various walks of life, and show that not all has yet been said in celebrity studies.

While discussion between the authors in the volume progresses, the readers will hopefully notice that they are frequently returning to unpacking the "ordinary/extraordinary divide." Questioning what "makes" a celebrity and how celebrity is controlled, dispersed and received are all related aspects branching out of our debate over celebrities as ordinary/extraordinary. Moreover, the intersecting elements of how celebrity is realised—through global media and/or the internet for example—are also drawn into a discussion of what is real and what is unreal in relation to celebrity construction, identity, and underscoring this, sincerity. This discussion is significant because it provides an avenue for exploring not just what celebrity is as a discursive construction, but also how this involves a complex interplay between celebrities, the media, and the audience.

Part 1 of the volume presents various ways and means of "Constructing Celebrity." The authors contributing to this section focus on individuals who have not only become symbols of and for their nations, but whose celebrity status has been fashioned, commercialised and politically utilised—not abused—by the public, authorities and various media. This section begins with

---

5   Mark Binelli, "Pope Francis: The Times They Are A-Changin," RollingStone, January 28, 2014, accessed February 5, 2014, http://www.rollingstone.com/culture/news/pope-francis-the-times-they-are-a-changin-20140128.
6   See Howard Chua-Eoan and Elizabeth Dias, "Pope Francis, The People's Pope," December 11, 2013, accessed February 5, 2014, http://poy.time.com/2013/12/11/person-of-the-year-pope-francis-the-peoples-pope/.

Amber Anna Colvin's chapter, "'The Big Fellow Is Dead!': Michael Collins as Celebrity and Nationalist Martyr," exploring the life and death of the Irish revolutionary.

Michael Collins as celebrity is a generated construction that sits at the intersection of loyalist and separatist discourses. While showing that his image remained recognisable long after his death, Colvin focuses on exploring the "vacuum that allowed new, post-mortem representations of his body to become famous."[7] Her analysis involves research conducted on both Irish and British newspapers; images of Collins after his death and of his funeral; as well as the ways Collins has been represented since his death, such as images of "local shrines" online, i.e. official websites, or films. Thus, Colvin shows that death is just a beginning, and even deceased celebrities may be used in national and political rhetoric, or even become a "brand."[8]

While Colvin discusses the branding of a celebrity martyr, Samita Nandy, in her "Mediating Bieber in Canada: Authenticating Nation in Fame," examines the contemporary ways in which online fame may express offline constructions of a nation. Through its focus on Justin Bieber, this chapter initiates a discussion of celebrity as a mediated negotiation of the ordinary and extraordinary, and, in particular, gives rise to questions regarding celebrity identity, sincerity, the role of the media, and the function of celebrity as a form of nationalist discourse.

Through her focus on Justin Bieber, Nandy investigates multifarious media constructions and their attempts at restoring various "social values of authenticity through ordinary expressions of national identity."[9] Her chapter shows how the tensions between Bieber's talent—extraordinary—and Canada—with its "ordinariness"—help to unfold the problematic questions of authenticity. Nandy's chapter, however, offers so much more than just a revision of Bieber's career; she presents an interdisciplinary study, necessary to understand "industrial practices and processes of fame in traditional and online media."[10] In the context of Canada, this is truly an innovative contribution to media and celebrity studies.

The two previous chapters discuss the way in which meaning is attributed to particular celebrities and their fame negotiated in a larger national context. In the third chapter, Sandra Mayer shifts the focus toward self-fashioning

---

7   See Colvin's contribution to this volume.
8   Ned Kelly's biography could, as a possible parallel, provide a unique and particularly dialogical exploration of celebrity, nation/nationalism, identity, function and temporality.
9   See Nandy's contribution to this volume.
10 Ibid.

celebrity. In her study of Harold Pinter and Elfriede Jelinek, and their Nobel Prize speeches, Mayer shows how these well-known individuals personally engaged in an act of self-fashioning, and, consequently, enforced their own interpretation of their characters on the public, as well as delivered political and artistic messages to the world. The Nobel Lectures provide a unique focus for the study of celebrity as a controlled discursive entity. Indeed, in Mayer's "Literary Celebrity, Politics and the Nobel Prize: The Nobel Lecture as an Authorial Self-Fashioning Platform," we can find analyses of issues such as *en-Nobeling*, authorial agency, the meaning of dichotomy between the public and the private self, the power of absence and "virtual presence," and the political power of literary celebrity.[11]

The previous section, particularly Mayer's chapter, has opened up an important thread within the volume, namely the power that celebrities have over the construction of their own stardom. While her chapter focuses on contemporary individuals, the self-fashioning processes she discusses can likewise be observed in Anna Fomichenko's contribution to this volume. Introducing Part 2, titled "(Re)Envisioning Stardom," Fomichenko in "Oscar Wilde's Long Afterlife: Victorian Celebrity and Its Transformations in Modern Culture" explains: "Although Oscar Wilde and his elaborate self-fashioning techniques were a product of the late Victorian era, they have undoubtedly created a basis for the phenomenon we call modern celebrity."[12] Indeed, she proves that, in comparison to many modern stars, Wilde does not seem to have an "expiry date." Fomichenko subsequently examines the various masks put on by Wilde to create his own legend, but also comments on the complex "author function," by which she means the actions of the actual person, his/her agents, theatrical managers, publishers, producers, etc., and, of course, the audience itself. To prove that the statement about Wilde's "durability" is not exaggerated and his self-fashioning processes have been utilised in our contemporary times, Fomichenko demonstrates how similar techniques have been appropriated by the surprisingly Wildean, David Bowie.

As can be assumed, Wilde was not as approachable as an average nineteenth-century individual, and the situation was no different with Bowie in the twenty-first century. How close one could get to their chosen idol and what relationships—real or—fans can establish with celebrities have become important subthemes within celebrity studies, and a central focus within the close relative: fan studies. While a significant group of cultural researchers, sociologists and psychologists examine the greatest, nationwide stars and

---

11 See Mayer's contribution to this volume.
12 See Fomichenko's contribution to this volume.

INTRODUCTION: (EXTRA)ORDINARY? 5

their fanbase, Jade Alexander, in "Touching Fame: Exploring Interactional Dynamics between Local Celebrities and Fans in Sydney's Roller Derby Scene," takes a look at the power of "local stars." Hers, however, is an in-depth and original study of flat track roller derby. Through this chapter, then, roller derby provides an avenue to examine and discuss not only a distinctly different formation of celebrity, but also how the increase in accessibility results in the fan/celebrity boundaries becoming less distinct. While introducing this type of sport and its rules, Alexander explores how female skaters negotiate fame, while also commenting on the players' insistence on staying "real" and maintaining "authenticity." The author gives us an insight into the various representations of fan/celebrity contact, especially the act of touching, or as Alexander explains it: physical contact "puts sport star celebrities within reach and as such separates roller derby from other sports."[13] For Alexander, this is particularly important since "the potential for contact in the roller derby scene can enable greater analysis of interactional dynamics and power relations present in fan and celebrity encounters, elements which are typically methodologically problematic in studies of global, mass-mediated celebrity formations."[14] Her chapter helps us answer questions, such as: How do we understand fame and celebrity in roller derby if skaters regard themselves, and are regarded by others, as "ordinary," "real," and or "average" people when they develop derby names and personas? What does this do to our understanding not only of celebrity as a cultural formation existing within a specific domain, but also to our appraisal of "fan"/"celebrity" relations?

Alexander's skaters seem to enjoy their fame and sustain a benevolent relationship with their fans. Their celebrity status is recognised, if on the local scale, because "[s]ocieties tend to honour their prominent citizens for unique contributions to the community and lifetime achievements,"[15] as noted by Mira Moshe, the author of the subsequent chapter. The adoration of crowds is one way of being rewarded for your contribution, but many societies bestow actual prizes on their "celebrated individuals." In the final chapter of Part 2, Moshe's "Celebrity Awards, Fan Communities and the Reconstruction of 'High' and 'Low' Cultures," compares two award ceremonies, the Israel Prize—held annually at the culmination of the Independence Day festivities in Jerusalem—and the "Gossip and Entertainment" internet site-driven "Israel Celeb Awards," happening on the same day. Moshe notes that what began as an attempt to sarcastically stress the gap between "high" and "low" culture eventually became a

---

13   See Alexander's contribution to this volume.
14   Ibid.
15   See Moshe's contribution to this volume.

"conceptual dialogue between 'admirers' and 'objectors,' replacing a discussion of cultural quality with an internal squabble among fans."[16] While analysing the complexities of both award ceremonies as well as the quality of the stars and the reactions of "fans" or admirers of the awarded individuals, Moshe suggests that these two competitions reinforce "the completeness of the fabric of Israeli society."[17]

Providing a comparative and contrasting review of celebrities, examining in detail the place of shame and "bad" behaviour in the media supported construction of celebrity in Israel, Moshe's chapter and the descriptions of walks of shame performed by some celebrities finishes the present volume but also opens a new thread in Celebrity Studies. Notoriety has been part and parcel of stardom, and recent decades have seen celebrities "behaving badly." In just a couple of years we have lost great individuals, and many more present celebrities seem to be testing the boundaries of morality, or, more so, the boundaries between life and death. These events spark off comments about the influence that celebrity has on individuals and point to the darker spots under the metaphorical limelight. All cases of misdemeanour and addiction-related deaths seem to overshadow the reports on the loss of great stars such as Shirley Temple and Nelson Mandela, the latter in particular representing the sphere where celebrity mixes with true heroism. For the world, these two "notable deaths," as they are denoted in the media, signify the end of an era; to scholars of stardom and fandom, these sad passings also make one re-consider the definitions of the meaning of (deserved) celebrity in the twenty-first century.

All of the chapters comprising the present volume show that there is still a lot to be done within celebrity studies. Considering the fact that the definitions of what or who (a) celebrity is are constantly being revised and expanded, and that these discussions are then intertwined with new studies on the nature of fandom, the editors of this volume humbly hope that the chapters included will allow other scholars to broaden their research on celebrity culture and the ways and means of achieving … and surviving fame.

Bibliography

Binelli, Mark. "Pope Francis: The Times They Are A-Changin." RollingStone, January 28, 2014. Accessed February 5, 2014. http://www.rollingstone.com/culture/news/pope-francis-the-times-they-are-a-changin-20140128.

---

16   Ibid.
17   Ibid.

Chua-Eoan, Howard, and Elizabeth Dias, "Pope Francis, The People's Pope." December 11, 2013. Accessed February 5, 2014. http://poy.time.com/2013/12/11/person-of-the-year-pope-francis-the-peoples-pope/.

Jersey Shore. Accessed February 5, 2014. http://www.mtv.com/shows/jersey_shore/season_2/series.jhtml.

Marshall, P. David, ed. *The Celebrity Culture Reader*. New York: Routledge, 2006.

Rojek, Chris. *Celebrity*. London: Reaktion Books, 2001.

Turner, Graeme. *Understanding Celebrity*. London: Sage, 2010.

PART 1

Constructing Celebrity

CHAPTER 1

"The Big Fellow Is Dead!": Michael Collins as Celebrity and Nationalist Martyr

Amber Anna Colvin

Abstract

Michael Collins, Irish revolutionary and political leader, was assassinated in 1922. After his death, his image remained recognisable, a type of "brand" that represented the Irish nation, both at home and abroad. The physical space left vacant by Collins created a vacuum that allowed new, post-mortem representations of his body to become famous. Collins was a celebrity during his own lifetime, but his fame truly grew when he was no longer alive to lay claim to his own image. Collins' image served as a means of continuing and contributing to the nationalist discourse in Ireland, particularly between the Irish and the British. The question should be asked: why, and how, is Collins still famous? This chapter discusses three sources for studying Collins as a celebrity martyr, and as his own personal "brand." First, placement of articles about Collins' death in both Irish and British newspapers evidence the spatial relationship between Collins and other news of the time, physically placing his textual image in particular spaces, allowing people to "see" his death, funeral, and influence through the mass media. Second, images of Collins after his death and of his funeral demonstrate the nationalist propaganda that came to surround his corporeal body. Finally, I examine the ways Collins has been represented since his death and the importance he still holds as a national celebrity and popular icon.

1   Introduction

"Ireland Mourns" and "Dublin Aghast!" roared headlines around the world in August, 1922. Michael Collins, Director of Intelligence for the IRA, Commander-in-Chief of the Irish Army, negotiator of the Home Rule Treaty and popularly known as "The Big Fellow," was assassinated by Anti-Treaty Irish forces in County Cork, Ireland. His death stunned the Irish nation, made national headlines throughout the world, and drew global attention to the Irish independence movement. His body was transported from Cork to Dublin where it lay in state for three days before being interred following a massive funeral in Dublin's Pro-Cathedral, where his "death portrait" was painted by a famous Irish artist. An estimated 500,000 people lined the streets for his funeral procession. Even today, there are numerous societies dedicated to Collins and annual commemorations of his death are still seen. Although opinions of Collins range from adoration to vehement hatred, his death and its circumstances elevate him to the role of a martyred national hero. Collins had, in death, become an international celebrity who represented Irish nationalism in ways unafforded in life.

Michael Collins was born in County Cork in 1890, around Clonakilty. At age 15, Collins took the British Civil Service examination and began work with the Royal Mail in 1906. He moved to London in 1910, working in an accountant's office until his return to Ireland in 1915. Sources agree that even while in London Collins was a part of the Irish Republican Brotherhood (IRB), a secret nationalist organisation, and he participated in the Easter Rising of 1916.[1] After the Easter Rising, Collins was a Sinn Fein leader and was elected to the Dial Eireann, the parliament of Ireland formed in opposition to the parliament in London. Appointed Minister of Finance in 1919, Collins was sent by Sinn Fein President Eamon de Valera to the 1921 treaty negotiations with Great Britain.[2]

Collins' death was tragic; he had recently accomplished near-independence for Ireland, but his actions had, however, led to the fracturing of his closest personal and professional relationships. He was to be married on the day of his death, but following the death of his friend and fellow revolutionary, Arthur Griffith, the wedding was postponed. For such a prominent Irishman to be killed by his own people, over a treaty with the British, just as the civil war seemed to be coming to a close, was the very definition of tragic. However, since Collins' death, his image has been used as an ideal for "Irishness," independence movements, romantic tragedies and nationalism. British and Irish newspapers presented Collins as a martyr, hero, and, foremost, as a celebrity whose own voice had been silenced, but whose memory and tragic death could be utilised to further nationalist discourse between Britain and Ireland in the 1920s. "Death portraits" of Collins, both in the form of photographs taken at his funeral and the famous painting by Sir John Lavery, as well as the physical descriptions given in newspapers created a body and image that could stand in for the "ideals" of various groups. I have previously examined how newspapers,

---

[1] Most sources, however, downplay his time in England and emphasise his early nationalist and revolutionary activities.

[2] This are widely known events, but for a more detailed history of Collins' pre-1921 career, see the bibliography. Eventually, despite the general feeling that de Valera had Collins killed (and, according to Coogan, directly admitted to it) de Valera was elected president of Ireland.

which were the most common and widely read form of media in the 1920s, used Collins' death as a commentary on the state of Irish and British relations and the ideas of imperialism and nation creation.[3] Here, I address the ways the physical presence of Collins was, and continues to be, evoked as a branding device.

How do celebrity and nationalism interact? For the purposes of this chapter, I define "celebrity" as an individual who is broadly known and recognised, both through image and deeds, and who has become a part of the social and cultural discourse of a given area and time period. One of the defining characteristics of celebrity is also the attempt to "preserve and publicize the image of an individual in the absence of his or her person" and is often historically connected to "performance" or presence in public spectacle. The argument has been made that Collins was actually a national hero, rather than a celebrity.[4] While I would certainly not equate Collins to modern media startlets, both categories fit the definition of celebrity I use: one that recognises the fluidity of the language of fame as well as the need for a broad category of analysis. The current, dominant definition of celebrity is skewed, often referring to celebrities involved in the entertainment industry rather than those who are famous or well-known for other reasons.

Celebrity has not, historically, always meant notoriety. For some, this has been the case, but fame can exist without scandal or irreverence. While Collins can certainly be labeled a national military and political hero, that term is not broad enough to encompass his image as it was presented following his death. He was not a national hero to the British, as they refused (as I discuss in my other work on Collins) to acknowledge Ireland as a nation. Collins was consistently associated with the Irish nation, but, to those who opposed the Anglo-Irish Treaty, he was not a hero at the time of his death. Celebrity, like art, "has many functions, social as well as individual."[5] In claiming that Collins was a national hero, rather than a celebrity, he and his image are forced into a box of meaning that allows little room for his continued fame. We can safely assume that everyone in Ireland, and most people in England, knew who

---

3 See my "'Ireland's Sorrow': Michael Collins, Celebrity and Nationalist Discourse in Irish and British Newspapers," in *The Performance of Celebrity: Creating, Maintaining and Controlling Fame*, ed. Amber Anna Colvin (Oxford: Inter-Disciplinary Press, 2013), 23–34.
4 I am grateful for the enlightening conversation at the 2nd Global Conference on Celebrity held in Lisbon, Portugal in March 2013 that gave rise to many of the ideas in this chapter, and for the helpful feedback I received on this project.
5 Hugh Trevor-Roper, *The Plunder of the Arts in the Seventeenth Century* (London: Thames and Hudson, 1972), 7.

Collins was. And, while he was a hero to many of these people, there is simply no way to empirically understand or analyse this phenomenon. Utilising a broad definition of celebrity is, I believe, the most accurate way to understand the entirety of Collins' impact after his death. Definitions of celebrity and hero vary greatly, but Collins was very clearly a celebrity in his own time, after his death, and even today.[6] As I will show, the sheer amount of page space and time devoted to Collins is indicative of his celebrity in 1922, much like the monuments and contemporary celebrations are testaments to his continued celebrity; in both instances, Collins' physical absence is acknowledged and replaced with recognisable memories, images, and monuments.

Samita Nandy, in examining the rise of Internet celebrities, particularly Justin Bieber, shows the importance of utilising widely available media and the importance of interaction with it. Although newspapers in the 1920s were very different from today's online community (where a representation of Collins is, actually, a presence, as I will discuss shortly), a degree of interaction with the media through letters to the editor and interviews with witnesses did exist. As Nandy points out in her chapter in this volume, "Mediating Bieber in Canada: Authenticating Nation in Fame," "expressions of national identity are common with purely offline stardom, but in the online cases, the expressions are further supported by the participation of fans."[7] Celebrities can achieve fame just by being recognisable, but, in the case of online forums, where participation is encouraged and necessary, fan support contributes to the creation and maintenance of celebrity. In Collins' case, newspapers accepted submissions and solicited interviews with witnesses, thus allowing for public participation.

This same idea can also apply to images of Collins, since the demand for these images drove, at least in part, their creation and content.[8] Newspapers, images, and the lingering remembrance and fame of Collins captured both the body and space of Collins as a celebrity and the participation of the general public in his fame. Justin Bieber, while famous for different actions, is a celebrity in many of the same ways as Collins: both are inextricably tied to a particular place, and thus become imbued with the ideals and implications of it. Although the sources presented here are far from being the complete works on Collins, a discussion of them will hopefully open doors to further scholarship, both on Collins and the representation of celebrity in general.

---

6 There is an overwhelming amount of books, articles, magazine spreads, movies, and references to Collins; I have tried to include many of the major works in the footnotes and bibliography.
7 Samita Nandy's contribution to this volume.
8 See Ibid.

2   Collins, Imperialism and the Home-Rule Treaty

Collins and Arthur Griffith were "the only two Ministers of the Provisional Government to impress their personalities on a public outside Ireland."[9] Collins was also considered a celebrity, even in India, after his death. Michael Silvestri notes that:

> In 1926, the *Daily Mail*'s correspondent in Calcutta reported that Bengali fascination with events in Ireland was greater than ever: Ireland has furnished the inspiration for the revolutionary movement in Bengal. Nothing interests the Bengali so much as the story of the rising against Dublin Castle, with its attendant ambuscades, assassinations, and street fighting. Nearly all the literature dealing the campaign of Michael Collins and his followers has been translated into the vernacular and is sold in native bookshops. The Bengali believes that if he adopts the same methods as the Irish Republicans he will achieve at last as great a measure of self-government.[10]

In the United States, the Irish community was outraged, and news of Collins' death was as prominent in major American newspapers as it was in British and Irish ones.[11] In the newspapers examined in this chapter, this celebrity status is also apparent. Collins was not simply famous, but was also an influential and inspiring figure that was easily recognised and understood by the general public. Both the Irish and British newspapers refer to Collins' death as a "personal loss," and a "loss" for either Ireland or the Irish nation.[12]

Any study of Irish and British nationalism must also address the idea of Ireland as an "imperial" possession. Ireland was, until 1922, a part of the United Kingdom and thus, neither technically or legally a colonial holding. However, historically, Ireland has been viewed as a territorial possession of England and their relationship was much akin to the relationship between Britain and its

---

9   *Manchester Guardian*, "The Men in the Irish Government," August 25, 1922, 4.
10 Michael Silvestri, *Ireland and India: Nationalism, Empire and Nation* (New York: Palgrave MacMillan, 2009), 58.
11 This comparison has not been fully examined as of this project, but it appears to be a project worthy of further study.
12 *Connaught Telegraph*, August 26, 1922, 3 and *Pall Mall Gazette*, August 28, 1922, 4; while the British newspapers do not describe Ireland as a nation, they do discuss "loss" many times.

colonial possessions.[13] Despite this, Ireland and Britain viewed each other as "them" or "the other." Collins was an enigma of sorts, being Irish while also having lived, worked, and negotiated a major piece of diplomacy in England; he was a revolutionary rabble-rouser, but had also sat at the table with the Prime Minister. His death, which newspapers were both eager and obliged to report on, can help historians understand the complicated relationship between Britain and Ireland.

The Anglo-Irish Treaty, signed December 6, 1921, was a treaty negotiated by the English Prime Minister, David Lloyd George and an Irish delegation consisting primarily of Collins and Arthur Griffith, Irish revolutionary and Collins' close friend. This treaty essentially made Ireland, with the exclusion of several of the northern counties, a self-governing dominion of Britain. Some British troops would remain in Ireland, and the British government would maintain a presence in several ports, while the northern counties would have the option to remain a part of Britain if they chose to do so, which they eventually did. Additionally, Ireland would be responsible for a part of Britain's debts at the time of the treaty. Creating the "Irish Free State," the Anglo-Irish Treaty led to a civil war between those who were in favor of the limited independence guaranteed by the treaty, and those who were against the significant compromises it entailed.

The story of the Irish Civil War has been told many times, but a brief overview of the conflict is helpful here. Upon returning to Ireland after the completion of the treaty, Griffith and Collins were met with dissatisfaction over the "Free State" agreement. Rather than an independent, autonomous republic, which would include all 32 Irish counties, Ireland remained, in name and fact, a dominion of the British. The Oath of Allegiance required of members of the Irish Parliament particularly displeased de Valera, who led the anti-Treaty movement:

> I...do solemnly swear true faith and allegiance to the Constitution of the Irish Free State as by law established and that I will be faithful to H.M. King George v., his heirs and successors by law, in virtue of the common citizenship of Ireland with Great Britain and her adherence to and membership of the group of nations forming the British Commonwealth of Nations.[14]

---

[13] Silvestri looks at Irish nationalism and Irish-Indian imperial relations in the late-nineteenth and early-twentieth centuries. He also examines the construction of Irishmen as British national heroes.

[14] Irish National Archives, "Documents on Irish Foreign Policy Series: Excerpts from the Anglo-Irish Treaty," accessed April 13, 2013, http://www.nationalarchives.ie/topics/anglo_irish/dfaexhib2.html.

De Valera had declined to attend the negotiations in their final stages, and Collins later stated that de Valera had set him up to take the blame for a flawed compromise. In any event, Irish forces and leaders split, with the Pro-Treaty provisional government headed by Collins and Griffith (who would oversee the transfer of power from British to Irish troops) and the Anti-Treaty forces, including most of the Irish Republican Army, led by de Valera. Although Collins hoped to avoid civil war, Anti-Treaty forces, popularly known as Irregulars, soon occupied the Four Courts in Dublin, leading to military action and the outbreak of a full-scale guerilla war.[15]

The war was bloody and convoluted, with neither side making enough progress to win outright. Griffith, President of the Dail Eireean (the Irish Parliament) died on August 12, 1922 of heart failure, and Collins was assassinated just ten days later. The war quickly deteriorated into an even bloodier conflict, with numerous executions of Anti-Treaty leaders. Eventually, the Anti-Treaty forces were forced to surrender on May 23, 1923. De Valera supported the ceasefire, stating that:

> Soldiers of the Republic, Legion of the Rearguard: The Republic can no longer be defended successfully by your arms. Further sacrifice of life would now be in vain and the continuance of the struggle in arms unwise in the national interest and prejudicial to the future of our cause. Military victory must be allowed to rest for the moment with those who have destroyed the Republic.[16]

The war did not truly end with this cease-fire, as hunger strikes followed the general election, in which the pro-Free State party won the majority of seats, and bitter resentment remained over the war and the Treaty. Collins was a crucial figure in the war, and his death haunted de Valera the rest of his life.

3 Placement of the Articles

When researching any historical source, the content is, of course, paramount, but the particulars of placement, conditions, author, and availability should be considered as well. The placement of articles in newspapers created a sense

---

15 The Four Courts, Dublin's primary court building, was seized during the 1916 Easter Rising, in which Collins also participated, and was partially destroyed during the Irish Civil War. The Four Courts has since reopened.

16 Thomas E. Hatchey, *The Irish Experience: A Concise History* (New York: M.E. Sharpe Publishing, 1996), 170–71.

of space for Collins; his presence dominated some papers, while in others, his existence and career were almost footnotes, often placed next to articles covering oppositional brutality. In both the Irish and British newspapers, articles on Collins' death appear alongside other news and advertisements. Most often, Irish newspapers devoted full pages to Collins' death, funeral, legacy, and so on, with few advertisements or personal letters of sympathy, or general news. Many British newspapers, however, often placed articles and advertisements around pieces on Collins that appear to represent him as an "exception to the rule" of sorts: while he is depicted as an upstanding citizen and leader, these articles appear alongside pieces on violence, ineptitude, and disorder, all emanating from the Irish.

The Times was particularly prone to this. Following a touching article on Collins' funeral procession is an article about a shooting in Belfast and another about men being gunned down in the streets of Dublin entitled "Callous Murders in Dublin: Two Men Shot in View of Crowd."[17] Next to another article about Collins is a piece on the bombing of the County Road Police Barracks in County Cork; four Irregulars were captured, but none of the National troops inside were killed. In this article, there are also mentions of a postal office bombing and several attacks on other sites in Cork. While these events did occur, the placement of their coverage is intriguing. Situated directly next to a description of the funeral itself, the headline "The Cork Attack on British Troops" appears, while under it is an article titled "British Soldier Shot in Belfast." Following these articles is a piece on train line disruptions due to rebellions in Ireland, another, titled "Attempt to Rob Officer of His Money," which details a particularly violent episode that resulted in the ambush of British troops and the death of several troops and Irregulars. Another piece, "Day of Mourning: Complete Stoppage of Work in Dublin," is situated next to "Rebel Ambushes in Cork: British Soldier Killed."[18] The article mentioned above, in which Collins was presented as "more than a lost leader to be mourned" and exceptional Irishman, appears next to "British Troops Attacked!"; this article describes, in great detail, the ambush of British soldiers by a group of Irregulars.[19] Next to an account of Collins' "Romantic Career," a denouncement of the "Cowardly Murderers" from the Prime Minister of Australia, Mr. Hughes, appears; it reads, "referring to the killing of Mr. Collins…it reveals to the world

---

17 "Callous Murders in Dublin: Two Men Shot in View of Crowd," *The Times*, August 24, 1922, 14.

18 "Day of Mourning: Complete Stoppage of Work in Dublin" and "Rebel Ambushes in Cork: British Soldier Killed," *The Times*, August 24, 1922, 7.

19 "British Troops Attacked!," *The Times*, August 24, 1922, 14.

the manner of men behind the so-called Republican Party in Ireland. They are a band of cowardly murderers. If any man had proved himself the friend and champion of Irish liberty, it was Michael Collins."[20]

At other times, Collins' death simply appears as everyday news; on one page, under "Stop-Press News," there is a notice about Collins' death, immediately followed by that week's golf scores.[21] Collins is featured alongside articles from America on "The Price of Prohibition," and next to advertisements for newspaper subscriptions and household items.[22] "Ireland's Sorrow," an article in the *Pall Mall Gazette,* is next to an article stating that there will be "No Change in Policy—Provided Ireland Observes Treaty."[23] Churchill was "not likely to curtail his holiday in Wales," despite Collins' death, according to the article.[24] On the first page of the same paper, "Ireland's Sorrow" appears to the side of the centre story which covers several large articles on recent tennis scores. The full title of the article reads "Ireland's Sorrow. Mr. Collins' Body in Dublin. 2 a.m. Scenes. Pipers' Lament and a Sniper's Shot," again indicating the violence and darkness surrounding Collins' death and the "Irish question."[25] The *Manchester Guardian* article on Collins' "Return to Dublin," lies next to a larger article on summer rainfall and its impact on the holiday season.[26] In the same issue, "A Brave and Wise Young Patriot" is found directly above an article about newspapers not reaching areas of Ireland because Irish rebels were burning them ("Dublin Papers Burned") and next to several articles describing various kidnappings and murders.[27] Although these could simply be layout decisions, they do invite speculation on their intent.

In Irish newspapers, very few advertisements appear at all on the pages with articles on Collins, as his funeral, death, legacy, and story tend to take up entire pages. Much of this can, of course, be attributed to Collins' Irish heritage

---

20 "Romantic Career," *The Times*, August 24, 1922, 14; two days later, on page 2, Ireland's problems are blamed on the "tyranny of the revolver" in the hands of roaming, "murderous gangs" who were inclined to "shoot with the intent to kill."
21 "Stop-Press News," *The Times*, August 24, 1922, 6.
22 While many Irish in the United States vehemently opposed Prohibition, this news is somewhat mundane compared to Collins' death.
23 "Ireland's Sorrow," *Pall Mall Gazette*, August 26, 1922, 8.
24 "No Change in Policy," *Pall Mall Gazette*, August 26, 1922, 8.
25 "Ireland's Sorrow," *Pall Mall Gazette*, August 26, 1922, 1.
26 "Collins' Return to Dublin," *Manchester Guardian*, August 25, 1922, 7.
27 "A Brave and Wise Young Patriot" and "Dublin Papers Burned," *Manchester Guardian*, August 25, 1922, 8.

and celebrity status in Ireland.[28] Articles that did appear adjacent to news of Collins' death tended to be of a non-political nature, such as the report from the board of a mental health hospital in the *Connaught Telegraph*.[29] Though Collins was certainly viewed as an important figure by the British newspapers, his presence in the "space" created for him, surrounded by other articles on Irish brutality, shows that he was viewed as the "exception to the rule" Irishman, a description that was a crucial part of British-Irish national discourse. This can be seen even more clearly in the descriptions of Collins in the newspapers.

4 Descriptions of Collins, His Death and His Funeral

The British newspapers portray Collins as the least savage of the savage Irish, truly the only Irishmen who could lead his wild and lawless compatriots. Physical descriptions of Collins abound in both the Irish and British papers which also show this contrast; Collins was often described as "tall," "impressive," and "military-like" in demeanor, all of which he surely was, but he was also seen as "brooding" and having "youthful vivacity" at the same time by various British papers.[30] These physical descriptions serve as part of Collins' celebrity to create a sense of his presence despite his physical absence, and both papers actively participated in this creation, albeit with different descriptions. While Collins certainly did not, in any surviving photographs, have a "heavy jowl," these descriptions of Collins and his death and funeral served to expand his fame.

Collins' masculinity was often noted, with articles referencing "his magnificent manhood' and his "vigorous" and "virile" character.[31] He had a "fearless heart,' with "no alien blood in his veins," which was "stilled in death," and his "brave, generous spirit…quitted its earthly home."[32] Before Collins' death, at the funeral of Arthur Griffith, he "looked in perfect health, and walked with firm tread and soldierly bearing, his face pale and stern, his head bent, his hands

---

28 Although he was, of course, "British" for the majority of his life, and did negotiate a major treaty that gave the British some major benefits in Ireland, both politically and financially.

29 "The Mental Hospital," *Connaught Telegraph*, August 26, 1922, 3.

30 These references are scattered throughout the British papers; most of the Irish papers agree, when they mention his appearance, but primarily focus on his nationality and grandeur, rather than physical appearance.

31 "The Late Michael Collins," *Southern Star*, August 26, 1922, 1 and "Checkmating Schemes of the British Militarists," *Freeman's Journal*, August 24, 1922, 6.

32 "An Appreciation by a Friend," *Southern Star*, August 26, 1922, 5, and "His Career in Brief," *Connacht Tribune*, August 26, 1922, 12.

gripping fast the large leather motor gloves he was carrying."[33] The *Southern Star* reports that, during his visit to Skibbereen a few days prior his death, he "was then in the pink of condition, bright, alert, erect, of fine soldierly bearing and withal a modesty that could not fail to win the admiration of the people."[34]

His size and virility were often seen as a contrast to the remaining Irish leadership. The *Manchester Guardian* noted that "One of Michael Collins's great assets was his physique. He was a splendid figure of a man, and of all the Dail leaders who had conduct of the treaty debates he alone matched his will to do things with an obvious physical ability to carry them through to the end"; the article goes on to list the ways in which de Valera and the rest of the Dail were not as physically impressive as Collins.[35] There is also the implication that the Irish need, or somehow intrinsically wanted, a large and masculine leader:

> One cannot avoid the feeling that sheer bigness of body gave Collins a pull. He looked the sort of man to lead young men. Who that is left has this particular qualification of leadership? Many of the present leaders of the Free State are journalists and poets and novelists, men who may do excellent work in the council chamber, but who are not likely to fill Ireland's need for a big romantic figure to follow. The man who comes to mind is General Sean McKeown, know all over Ireland as "the chivalrous blacksmith of Ballinalee." General McKeown, one feels would do well at the head of the Irish Army. He, more than any man whose name occurs to one, has that bluff flavour which the Irish like, and one recalls the personal touch of friendship and affection which marked recently his reception in his own part of Ireland. There is a little of legend about him already, and legend is the gift of the gods to a military leader. As would be expected in one of his craft, General McKeown is a man of brawn and bone, robust and muscular.[36]

Perhaps even more important are the ways the Irish and British newspapers described the site of Collins' assassination. This relation of a celebrity to a place, or the idea of a place, is seen in other instances as well; Nandy argues that, "popular representations show that authenticity of famous Canadian personalities is often established through intimacy with Northern nature," and

---

33 "Dublin Aghast," *Southern Star*, August 26, 1922, 4.
34 "Sorrow in Skibbereen," *Southern Star*, August 26, 1922, 5.
35 "The New Commander-in-Chief," *Manchester Guardian*, August 25, 1922, 6.
36 Ibid.

Collins' association with the place of his death and funeral serves the same purpose.[37] Nandy also notes that tying celebrities or iconic brands (like Justin Bieber or Tim Hortons) to a physical space allows them to, "authenticate the territorially bounded (...) nation as a home or homeland of its citizens."[38]

In the *Pall Mall Gazette* article "Ireland's Sorrow," Collins' funeral and assassination were described in great detail, drawing primarily from the experiences of a man who had been with Collins during the attack, a "boyish figure wearing a ragged civilian coat and tweed cap perched jauntily on the back of his head," who carried a "Lewis gun, the same Lewis gun...that poured a hail of lead into Michael Collins's attackers."[39] He told his story in a "shy, diffident manner," painting a picture of the scene: "The car in which the C.-in-C. [Commander-in-Chief] was riding...was the first to meet the fire of the ambushers. There at least 250 of them against 12 of us."[40] Collins, according to this account, ordered his driver to stop so he could engage the attackers, who ambushed Collins' group almost immediately after passing through a village with a "deadly cross-machine-gun fire."[41] Similar descriptions are found in the *Connaught Telegraph* article "How General Collins Died."

Collins' funeral was the subject of several articles in both the Irish and British papers. In the *Connacht Tribune*'s "Appreciation by Governor Cox," the reactions to the funeral outside of Dublin are described. "Throughout Connacht, as in other provinces, there were everywhere signs of public mourning," the *Tribune* stated, and "from all parts of the country come reports indicating the feeling which has been aroused by the death of General Collins."[42] In the *Southern Star*'s report on Michael Collins' brother, John Collins, they note that when Michael Collins' body arrived in Dublin, "his fiancée and...sister were amongst the first to enter the chapel," where the "lid of the coffin had been removed and the full-length view of the dead leader" was visible.[43]

The *Manchester Guardian* describes Collins' funeral as "The greatest funeral that any Irish leader has ever had," and notes that, "although the funeral to-day was military, it was not of the blood-stirring kind to which we are accustomed in England. In the middle of the city...the enormous procession went silently

---

37 See Nandy, "Mediating Bieber in Canada: Authenticating Nation in Fame," in this volume.
38 Ibid.
39 "Ireland's Sorrow," *Pall Mall Gazette*, August 26, 1922, 8.
40 Ibid.
41 Ibid.
42 "In the Country" and "A Western Threat," *Connacht Tribune*, August 26, 1922, 3.
43 "Brother of the Dead Chief," *Southern Star*, August 26, 1922, 5.

on its way to Glasnevin between vast, silent, undemonstrative crowds."[44] The *Manchester Guardian* also describes the return of Collins' body to Dublin:

> The body of General Collins was brought back to Dublin before it was light this morning…As the ship was docked the "Last Post" was blown by buglers, and the stately and melancholy notes were followed by the muffled sound of gunfire from snipers operating in some other part of the city. The coffin was carried down to the gangway by staff officers and placed on the carriage of an eighteen-pounder gun. It was covered with the Irish tricolour, and passed into position between two ranks of Dublin Guards, who reversed their arms and led a long and strange procession through the empty streets to St. Vincent's Hospital. The shooting in the distance still went on.[45]

These descriptions have several interesting aspects. First, the implication that Collins' funeral was far removed from any seen in England, because the Irish did not possess a "blood-stirring" type of patriotism; also, the references to "undemonstrative crowds" represents a clear insult to the Irish. Although there are many references to the difference between the two nations in the Irish papers, this is one of the more blatant "us vs. them" comparisons seen. Also, in mentioning the gunfire in Dublin twice, the author seemed to want to show Dublin as a war-zone, and Ireland as a country torn by war. While not wholly untrue, the emphasis here seems out of place for a report on a deceased leader—it reads more like a report on the state of the war. These articles served dual purposes. They were news, but with a propagandistic slant.

5   Paintings and Photographs

Paintings and photographs of Collins' corpse, his funeral, and of the site of his assassination also played a major role in making Collins a martyred national celebrity. These images were widely circulated and prominently displayed, and continue to be displayed today. Also, in the case of the photographs, we can gain a sense of the scope of Collins funeral and public mourning, and how his funeral represented Collins' role as a celebrity which was appropriated for national and political purposes. Studies of the body and its role in history are not new, but Collins has rarely been examined in this light. "Through mass

---

44   "Michael Collins's Funeral," *Manchester Guardian*, August 28, 1922, 6.
45   "Collins' Return to Dublin," *Manchester Guardian*, August 25, 1922, 3.

culture the body became a text upon which messages can be inscribed, literally or figuratively, and then disseminated to the public,'" and Collins' body served to propagate national discourse and the idealisation of "Irishness."[46] Paige Reynolds cites Michael Warner who "claims, to be public in the West is to have an 'iconicity,' or a body whose image can be displayed to the masses through print and visual media."[47] Examining images of Collins after his death, then, can contribute much to the discussion of his post-mortem impact on the Irish consciousness.

The most famous, and likely the most widely seen, image of Collins is the famous "death portrait" of the fallen leader painted by Sir John Lavery. Lavery had painted Collins as a member of the Treaty delegation, and, when Collins died, it was Lavery, tangentially involved in the Irish independence movement, who painted his image. This painting, "Michael Collins (Love of Ireland)," today hangs in the Hugh Lane Gallery in Dublin. Approximately two feet by two and a half feet in size, the image depicts the dead Collins is dressed in his military uniform, pale and ashen in death, and covered with the Irish tricolour and a cross; the words "Love of Ireland" are etched above his body against a black background. The painting is dark, with the face of Collins and the flag as the brightest focal points. The Hugh Lane Gallery notes that, "this image of Collins in death has a majestic quality that is underscored by the purple pillow on which his head rests. The emblems of the crucifix and tricolour emphasize that Collins died for his country."[48] This painting has clear nationalist overtones, and shows the association of Collins and his physical presence (as his body is so prominently tied to Irish nationalism) to the Irish cause; that it was painted by a famous and popular painter makes it even more important and relevant.

Photographs were rarely reproduced in the newspapers; this was cost prohibitive, and, as shown, newspapers relied on fast-breaking stories with descriptions standing in for images. In most images of Collins, he is shown in military dress, often armed; in some, he is shown riding the streets of London on his bicycle. Recently, the last known photo of Collins before his death came to light, with Collins riding in the back of an open car. The same photographer, 18-year-old Agnes Hurley, also captured the only known image of the ambush

---

46 Paige Reynolds, "Modernist Martyrdom: The Funerals of Terence MacSwiney," *Modernism/Modernity* 9, no. 4 (November, 2002): 538.

47 Ibid., 537, citing Michael Warner, "The Mass Public and the Mass Subject," in *The Phantom Public Sphere*, ed. Bruce Robbins (Minneapolis: University of Minneapolis Press, 1993), 242.

48 Hugh Lane Municipal Gallery of Modern Art, "Society and Politics 18 September–3 November 1996," accessed April 13, 2013, http://emuseum.pointblank.ie/online_catalogue/work-detail.php?objectid=1033, 222.

site at Beal Na Blath, in which a small scrap of fabric, thought to be the bloody collar from Collins' shirt, is visible.[49] Several photographs from his funeral exist as well; these show the multitude of mourners, flowers, and emotions present that day. Although these photos and image were not as pervasive as the newspaper reports, they were available to be seen in galleries, in the case of Lavery's painting, and images of Collins were put on postcards and memorial cards, and were surely displayed in public places and private homes. These images, and their visibility and proliferation, impacted the continuation of Collins' celebrity from 1922 to the present day.

6   The Collins "Brand" Today

The nationalist celebrations and commentaries on Collins did not end in 1922, although the largest public celebrations were held that year. Rather, Collins' life and death are still commemorated today, and, as with the newspapers and art that appeared near the time of his death, "fan" participation remains crucial. The Collins 22 Society continues to propagate the idea that, "the prevailing ideology and value system of modern politics is failing people in so many ways… Michael Collins offers us a vision of a healthy society based on our God-given human dignity."[50] Their Mission Statement includes aspiring to the life principles of Collins, campaigning for a statue of Collins to be erected by the state in front of Leinster House by 2022, and to "extend the influence of Michael Collins by promoting an active interest in his life, his work, his writings, and in the ethos he bequeathed to the Irish people, primarily among the youth of Ireland."[51] This society, founded in 2002, has branches in Ireland and the United Kingdom, and allows for international membership.[52] Even here, Collins' life is being used as part of a "national" movement, one that commemorates his death and actively strives to celebrate both his life and martyrdom.

The official Michael Collins Memorial Centre, in Castleview, Clonakilty in County Cork, Collins' birthplace, is an entire museum and experience dedicated to Collins. At the Centre:

---

49   "Pictured Hours Before His Assassination: Last Photograph of IRA Leader Michael Collins Found in an Attic After 90 Years," *Daily Mail*, 4 December 2012, accessed April, 13 2013, http://www.dailymail.co.uk/news/article-2242724/Never-seen-pictures-final-hours-IRA-leader-Michael-Collins-emerged-spending-90-years-forgotten-attic.html.
50   The Collins 22 Society, accessed April 13, 2013, http://generalmichaelcollins.com/.
51   Ibid.
52   See: http://www.generalmichaelcollins.com/membership/.

As soon as visitors arrive at the Michael Collins Centre, they proceed to the Cottage/theatre. A twenty-minute audio/ visual explores the Big Fella's childhood, his family history, his school days and the important Collins' sites around Clonakilty. A guide then continues the presentation, using slides, large photographs or film clips, the visitor is taken through the 1916 rebellion, War of Independence, Treaty talks and the Civil War. The tragic death of Michael Collins at Bael na mBlath and his Legacy are also discussed. The presentation ends with a guided tour of the ambush trail, a life size replica of an ambush site complete with Crossley Tender and replica of Michael Collins, famous Rolls Royce Armoured Car, "Sliabh Na mBan." Here the events at Beal na Blath and the history of the vehicles in the Collins convoy are explained in more detail. Visitors can then return to the Cottage/Theatre to view the exhibition of photographs, documents and militaria.[53]

According to the website, reenactments of the ambush also take place at the replica of the ambush site, as do a "Michael Collins" tour (which appears very popular, as it must be booked several months in advance in the summer), and a "War of Independence" tour. A statue of Collins, created in 2001 and the first in the world according to the Centre, is also present in Clonakilty.[54]

Other groups, like the Irish Volunteers Commemorative Organisation, founded in 1913 in reaction to the anti-Home Rule Ulster Volunteer Force, have several articles on their websites about Collins, and there are numerous memorial "shrines" in Ireland dedicated to Collins.[55] Collins' grave is almost continuously covered in flowers and remembrance ceremonies take place at Glasnevin Cemetery; also, a yearly memorial takes place at Bael na mBlath; in 2009, Former President of Ireland and UN High Commissioner for Human Rights Mary Robinson gave the oration at this memorial.[56] Robinson said "Ireland more than ever now needs a visionary, like Michael Collins, who can lead us out of our current economic crisis and help engender a more equitable

---

[53] The Michael Collins Memorial Centre, accessed April 13, 2013, http://www.michaelcollinscentre.com/the-centre.html.

[54] Memorial Centre. Over £100,000 was raised for this statue, and Liam Neeson attended the unveiling, along with 7500 others.

[55] Irish Volunteers Commemorative Organisation, accessed April 13, 2013, http://irishvolunteers.org/.

[56] Wikipedia.org, "Michael Collins," accessed April 13, 2013, http://en.wikipedia.org/wiki/Michael_Collins_(Irish_leader); and Coppeen Archaeological Cultural Historical Society, accessed April 13, 2013, http://www.coppeenheritage.com/2009/08/24/beal-na-mblath-commemoration.

and fair society in Ireland." This event was also attended by Collins' grandniece, Helen Hoare, who spoke in praise of Robinson and her achievements for Irish society.[57] Hundreds of images of smaller, local shrines exist on the internet, both through official websites and the public photo albums of those who have visited them.[58]

Although I have thus far been unable to find any memorials to Collins outside of Ireland, a branch of the 1922 Society does operate in the United States. Today, he has a growing presence in film and his image and name continue to be a recognisable "brand." In 1996, *Michael Collins* was released. Academy Award winner Liam Neeson portrayed Collins, along with Oscar winner Julia Roberts as Kitty Kiernan and Alan Rickman as Eamon de Valera, and a young Jonathan Rhys-Myers, later of "The Tudors" fame, as Collins' assassin; the film was very popular, grossing over $16 million world-wide and becoming the top grossing film in Ireland of all time. One of the most interesting aspects of the DVD release was the physical disc. It was released with two sides: one side containing the movie and the other the special features. One side depicted Collins as a rebel, fighting the British military, and the other had Collins as an officer fighting the rebels. The irony of Collins' position comes through well in the movie, but is especially clear on the disc.[59]

Several other films have been made about Collins' life, and he is referenced in songs, plays, documentaries, and several historical novels.[60] There is a "Michael Collins" brand of whiskey, which features his silhouette on his famous bicycle and his signature on the bottle.[61] There is also a musical based on Collins' life, revolutionary activities, and death.[62] In 2012, two Irish college students visiting the United States traveled the country with a life-size, cardboard cutout of Collins, documenting "his" adventures on their Facebook page, "Michael Collins Adventures" and on Twitter, using the name "@micksadventures." "Collins" took in a baseball game, road in a cab, and went to several

---

57   Coppeen Archaeological Cultural Historical Society.
58   The Collins 22 Society's United States chapter also has a Facebook page, "Collins 22 Society US," accessed April 25, 2013, https://www.facebook.com/pages/Michael-Collins-22-Society/110157405730900.
59   IMDB.com, "Michael Collins," accessed April 13, 2013, http://www.imdb.com/title/tt0117039/trivia.
60   One of popular novelist Leon Uris' most poignant novels, *Trinity*, does not reference Collins directly, but its main character appears to share several physical and personality traits with Collins.
61   "Michael Collins Irish Whiskey," accessed April 13, 2013, http://michaelcollinswhiskey.com/.
62   "Michael Collins Musical," accessed April 13, 2013, http://www.michaelcollinsmusical.com/.

pubs.[63] One of the images on the "Michael Collins Adventures" Facebook page is the cutout "holding" a sign which reads "If this photo gets 10,000 Likes, I'll go back to London and Renegotiate the Treaty."[64] This comedic enterprise further supports the argument made here that Collins was, and continues to be, both a recognisable "brand" and a celebrity whose post-mortem fame is fuelled by "fan" participation. Finally, a new photograph of Collins, most likely the last before his death, was discovered, along with photos of the ambush scene the next day. These present day references to Collins illustrate the continued importance and relevance of Collins' image.

7 Conclusions

Collins' contributions to Irish independence and Irish nationalism cannot be underestimated. His celebrity status reached epic proportions after his death, and he is still a rallying point for Irish pride and new generations of Irish activists. What, then, can be gained from a closer look at his post-mortem fame and the ways in which his memory was used in the most popular media of his day, the newspaper, and in the images his death inspired? While Irish and British hostilities are generally dormant at this moment, the last century has seen a huge amount of death, destruction, and loss based on this conflict. By understanding more clearly the origins of Collins' mythical status and his enshrinement as a national hero, these conflicts can be more easily understood and their origins more clearly analysed. In "We Must Forget the Fantasies of the Past and Face the Tough Truth," Eoghan Harris argues for viewing the heroes of Ireland's past as heroes, but not as mythical figures that can "fix" modern-day problems.[65]

This chapter represents an attempt to more fully understand the world, with its various tensions, loyalties, and customs, in which Collins lived, fought, and died. While an examination of Collins as a post-mortem celebrity used in nationalist discourse may do little to ease ongoing conflicts, and should not

---

63 World Irish, "J1 Students Take Michael Collins Cut-out on Tour," accessed July 31, 2013, http://www.worldirish.com/story/1428-j1-students-take-michael-collins-cut-out-on-us-tour. Also see "Michael Collins Adventures," https://www.facebook.com/MichaelCollinsAdventures?fref=ts and "Mick's Adventures," https://twitter.com/micksadventures, both accessed July 31, 2013.

64 World Irish, "Michael Collins uses latest Facebook fad for Anglo-Irish treaty Renegotiations," accessed July 31, 2013, http://www.worldirish.com/story/22056-michael-collins-uses-latest-facebook-fad-for-anglo-irish-treaty-renegotiations.

65 Eoghan Harris, "We Must Forget the Fantasies of the Past and Face the Tough Truth," Irish Independent Online, accessed April 13, 2013, http://www.independent.ie/opinion/analysis/we-must-forget-the-fantasies-of-the-past-and-face-the-tough-truth-2880075.html.

be seen as an attempt to undermine a truly great leader's accomplishments, it can provide us with a crucial understanding of the world in 1922 and today, both of which have been influenced by "the Big Fellow." As the Irish Publicity Department stated on 23 August 1922:

> The greatest and bravest of our countrymen has been snatched from us at the moment when victory smiled through the clouds upon the uprising of the nation to which he dedicated all the powers of his magnificent manhood... . He has been slain to our unutterable grief and loss, but he cannot die. He will live in the rule of the people which he gave his great best to assert and confirm, and which his colleagues undertake as a solemn charge to maintain.[66]

Michael Collins is just one example of celebrities who become ideals and allegorical figures after their deaths. While a living celebrity can always disappoint or go against the wishes of the public or the nation, a deceased celebrity can be used in multiple ways and by many different groups. Collins was used as a tragic figure, as seen in the multiple references to the Treaty, his fiancée, and his vigor and masculinity in life. He was used as a political tool in the media by Irish and British newspapers, which compared him to the remaining leadership and held him as the ideal. In a *Manchester Guardian* article on the remaining leadership, Collins was described as "one whose name would live in history."[67] That has clearly been the case. Collins has also been used by generations of Irish, British, and international consumers of popular culture and activists, as continued relevance and recognisability show. Much research remains to be done on the celebrity of Collins and the roles of nationalism and martyrdom in the creation and perpetuation of celebrity around the world, but this chapter aims to contribute to the current discussion and open a new dialogue on the historical celebrity.

Bibliography

"A Brave and Wise Young Patriot" and "Dublin Papers Burned." *Manchester Guardian*, August 25, 1922, 8.
"An Appreciation by a Friend." *Southern Star*, August 26, 1922, 5.

---

66 This was in many papers, including the *Connacht Tribune* ("He Cannot Die," August 26, 1922, 12) and the *Freeman's Journal* ("Michael Collins Will Live in the Rule of the People," August 24, 1922, 5), where it was published in Gaelic.
67 "Mr. J.H. Thomas on Collins," *Manchester Guardian*, August 25, 1922, 6.

Anderson, Benedict. *Imagined Communities*. New York: Verso, 2006.
"A Western Threat." *Connacht Tribune*, August 26, 1922, 3.
"British Troops Attacked!" *The Times*, August 24, 1922, 14.
"Brother of the Dead Chief." *Southern Star*, August 26, 1922, 5.
"Callous Murders in Dublin: Two Men Shot in View of Crowd." *The Times*, August 24, 1922, 14.
"Checkmating Schemes of the British Militarists." *Freeman's Journal*, August 24, 1922, 6.
Colley, Linda. *Britons: Forging the Nation 1707–1837*. New Haven: Yale University Press, 1992.
"Collins' Return to Dublin." *Manchester Guardian*, August 25, 1922, 7.
Collins, Michael. *The Path to Freedom*. Boulder, Colorado: Roberts Rinehart Publishers, 1996.
Colvin, Amber Anna. "'Ireland's Sorrow': Michael Collins, Celebrity and Nationalist Discourse in Irish and British Newspapers." In *The Performance of Celebrity: Creating, Maintaining and Controlling Fame*, edited by Amber Anna Colvin, 23–34. Oxford: Inter-Disciplinary Press, 2013.
Coogan, Tim Pat. *Michael Collins: The Man Who Made Ireland*. Boulder, CO: Roberts Rinehart Publishers, 1996.
Coogan, Tim Pat. *The IRA*. New York: Palgrave Macmillan, 2002.
Coogan, Tim Pat. *1916: The Easter Rising*. Washington: Phoenix, 2005.
Coogan, Tim Pat. *Eamon de Valera: The Man Who Was Ireland*. New York: Sterling Publishers, 1999.
Coppeen Archaeological Cultural Historical Society. "Bael na Mblath Commemoration." Accessed April 13, 2013. http://www.coppeenheritage.com/2009/08/24/beal-na-mblath-commemoration.
"Day of Mourning: Complete Stoppage of Work in Dublin" and "Rebel Ambushes in Cork: British Soldier Killed." *The Times*, 2 August 24, 1922, 7.
De Valera, Terry. *A Memoir*. Dublin: Currach Press, 2004.
Doherty, Gabriel, and Dermot Keogh. "'Sorrow But No Despair: The Road is Marked': The Politics of Funerals in Post-1916 Ireland." In *Michael Collins and the Making of the Irish State*, edited by Gabriel Doherty, and Dermot Keogh, 186–201. Cork: Mercier Press, 2006.
"Dublin Aghast." *Southern Star*, August 26, 1922, 4.
Ferriter, Diammond. *Judging Dev: A Reassessment of the Life and Legacy of Eamon de Valera*. Dublin: Royal Irish Academy Publishing, 2007.
Gleeson, James. *Bloody Sunday: How Michael Collins's Agents Assassinated Britain's Secret Service in Dublin on November 21, 1920*. Guilford, CT: The Lyons Press, 2004.
Hannigan, David. *De Valera in America: The Rebel President and the Making of Irish Independence*. New York: Palgrave Macmillan, 2010.

Harris, Eoghan. "We Must Forget the Fantasies of the Past and Face the Tough Truth." Irish Independent Online. Accessed April 13, 2013. http://www.independent.ie/opinion/analysis/we-must-forget-the-fantasies-of-the-past-and-face-the-tough-truth-2880075.html.

Hatchey, Thomas E. *The Irish Experience: A Concise History*. New York: M.E. Sharpe Publishing, 1996.

"He Cannot Die." *Connacht Tribune*, August 26, 1922, 12.

"His Career in Brief." *Connacht Tribune*, August 26, 1922, 12.

Hittle, J.B.E. *Michael Collins and the Anglo-Irish War: Britain's Counterinsurgency Failure*. Dulles, VA: Potomac Books, 2011.

Hugh Lane Municipal Gallery of Modern Art. "Exhibition Catalogue: Society and Politics 18 September–3 November 1996." Accessed April 13, 2013. http://emuseum.pointblank.ie/online_catalogue/work-detail.php?objectid=1033.

"In the Country." *Connacht Tribune*, August 26, 1922, 3.

"Ireland's Sorrow." *Pall Mall Gazette*, August 26, 1922, 8.

Irish National Archives. "Documents on Irish Foreign Policy Series: Excerpts from the Anglo-Irish Treaty." Accessed April 13, 2013. http://www.nationalarchives.ie/topics/anglo_irish/dfaexhib2.html.

Irish Volunteers Commemorative Organisation. Accessed April 13, 2013. http://irishvolunteers.org/.

Kee, Robert. *The Green Flag: A History of Irish Nationalism*. New York: Penguin Books, 1972.

Kenneally, Ian. *The Paper Wall: Newspapers and Propaganda in Ireland, 1919–1921*. Wilton: The Collins Press, 2008.

Mackay, James. *Michael Collins: A Life*. London: Mainstream Publishing, 1996.

MacManus, M.J. *Eamon de Valera*. Dublin: MacManus Press, 2007.

"Michael Collins." IMDB.com. Accessed April 13, 2013. http://www.imdb.com/title/tt0117039/trivia.

"Michael Collins Adventures." Accessed July 31, 2013. https://www.facebook.com/MichaelCollinsAdventures?fref=ts.

"Michael Collins Irish Whiskey." Accessed April 13, 2013. http://michaelcollinswhiskey.com/.

"Michael Collins Musical." Accessed April 13, 2013. http://www.michaelcollinsmusical.com/.

"Michael Collins Will Live in the Rule of the People." *Freeman's Journal*, August 24, 1922, 5.

"Michael Collins's Funeral." *Manchester Guardian*, August 28, 1922, 6.

"Mick's Adventures." Accessed July 31, 2013. https://twitter.com/micksadventures.

"Mr. J.H. Thomas on Collins." *Manchester Guardian*, August 25, 1922, 6.

Neeson, Eoin. *The Life and Death of Michael Collins*. Cork: The Mericer Press, 1968.

"No Change in Policy." *Pall Mall Gazette*, August 26, 1922, 8.

O'Connor, Frank. *Death in Dublin: Michael Collins and the Irish Revolution*. New York: Doubleday, Doran & Company, Inc., 1937.

"Pictured Hours Before His Assassination: Last Photograph of IRA Leader Michael Collins Found in an Attic After 90 Years." *Daily Mail*, December 4, 2012. Accessed April 13, 2013. http://www.dailymail.co.uk/news/article-2242724/Never-seen-pictures-final-hours-IRA-leader-Michael-Collins-emerged-spending-90-years-forgotten-attic.html.

Regan, John M. *The Irish Counter-Revolution 1921–1936: Treatyite Politics and Settlement in Independent Ireland*. New York: St. Martin's Press, 1999.

Reynolds, Paige. "Modernist Martyrdom: The Funerals of Terence MacSwiney." *Modernism/Modernity* 9, No. 4 (November 2002): 535–559.

Roach, Joseph. "Celebrity Erotics: Pepys, Performance, and Painted Ladies." In *Politics, Transgression, and Representation at the Court of Charles II*, edited by Julia Marciari Alexander, and Catharine MacLeod, 233–51. New Haven: Yale University Press, 2007.

"Romantic Career." *The Times*, August 24, 1922, 14.

Silvestri, Michael. *Ireland and India: Nationalism, Empire and Nation*. New York: Palgrave MacMillan, 2009.

"Sorrow in Skibbereen." *Southern Star*, August 26, 1922, 5.

"Stop-Press News." *The Times*, August 24, 1922, 14.

The Collins 22 Society. Accessed April 13, 2013. http://generalmichaelcollins.com/.

The Collins 22 Society's United States Chapter. Accessed April 13, 2013. https://www.facebook.com/pages/Michael-Collins-22-Society/110157405730900.

"The Late Michael Collins." *Southern Star*, August 26, 1922, 1.

"The Mental Hospital." *Connaught Telegraph*, August 26, 1922, 3.

The Michael Collins Memorial Centre. Accessed April 13, 2013. http://www.michaelcollinscentre.com/the-centre.html.

"The New Commander-in-Chief." *Manchester Guardian*, August 25, 1922, 6.

Trevor-Roper, Hugh. *The Plunder of the Arts in the Seventeenth Century*. London: Thames and Hudson, 1972.

Turpin, John. "Visual Marianism and National Identity in Ireland 1920–1960." In *Art, Nation and Gender: Ethnic Landscapes, Myths and Mother-Figures*, edited by Tricia Cusack, and Sighle Bhreathnach-Lynch, 67–78. Burlington, VT: Ashgate Publishing Company, 2003.

Unowsky, Daniel. *The Pomp and Politics of Patriotism: Imperial Celebrations in Habsburg Austria, 1848–1916*. West Lafayette, IN: Purdue University Press, 2005.

Warner, Michael. "The Mass Public and the Mass Subject." In *The Phantom Public Sphere*, edited by Bruce Robbins. Minneapolis: University of Minneapolis Press, 1993.

Wikipedia. "Michael Collins." Accessed April 13, 2013. http://en.wikipedia.org/wiki/Michael_Collins_Irish_leader.

Wilson, Kathleen. *The Island Race: Englishness, Empire, and Gender in the Eighteenth Century*. New York: Routledge, 2003.

World Irish. "J1 Students Take Michael Collins Cut-out on Tour." Accessed July 31, 2013a. http://www.worldirish.com/story/1428-j1-students-take-michael-collins-cut-out-on-us-tour.

World Irish. "Michael Collins Uses Latest Facebook Fad for Anglo-Irish Treaty Renegotiations." Accessed July 31, 2013b. http://www.worldirish.com/story/22056-michael-collins-uses-latest-facebook-fad-for-anglo-irish-treaty-renegotiations.

CHAPTER 2

Mediating Bieber in Canada: Authenticating Nation in Fame

Samita Nandy

Abstract

This chapter examines ways in which online fame expresses offline constructions of a nation. These expressions are often articulated through ordinariness of a nation in contrast to the extraordinary talent or heroism of a celebrity. Since maintenance of territorial boundaries has been the traditional premise for a unifying national identity, the global reach of online fame may threaten national interests of media corporations. Nevertheless, corporations often reclaim national identity of celebrities for development of national and transnational brands. The expression of a dominant national identity also helps fans to identify with celebrities, both online and offline. This chapter maps the relation between fame and nation, and uses a case study of pop star Justin Bieber to show specific ways in which his national identity is accepted, negotiated or subverted in online and traditional media. In particular, this chapter shows how the tensions between Bieber's extraordinary talent and the ordinariness of his nation unfold questions of authenticity. The use of Justin Bieber's authenticity not only maintains his fame but also Canada as his homeland and a frontier nation in a colonialist context. To understand organisational and corporate ways of articulating national identity in fame, the chapter recognises the need to focus on industrial production as well as the discursive construction of celebrities.

1   Celebrities and Nation

The notion of celebrity as a national hero can be traced back to the rise of the Industrial Revolution. At that time, decline of organised religion, new conditions of capitalism and democratisation of society replaced earlier forms of monarchy. In this context, mass media played a significant role in constructing celebrities as enablers of social mobility that was nearly absent in the past. Individuals identify with these media constructions as achievable forms of freedom on a personal level. At the same time, media help inscribing social values in celebrity constructions that have been meaningful for national cohesion on a collective level. These expressions are often related to authenticity that has been lost in the industrialisation of a nation. However, media constructions attempt to restore social values of authenticity through ordinary expressions of national identity. This ordinariness contrasts extraordinary talent or heroism of a celebrity in a nation. It is a paradox that creates and sustains desire of a celebrity and, more importantly, the nation in which the celebrity is constructed. Amber Anna Colvin defined the celebrity as "an individual who is broadly known and recognised, both through image and deeds, and is a part of the social and cultural discourse of a given area and time period."[1] She explained that a celebrity is also the attempt to preserve and publicise the image of an individual in the absence of his or her person and is often historically connected to performance or presence in public spectacles. The understanding of celebrities as extraordinary performers of public spectacles sets theoretical grounds for this chapter to explain Justin Bieber as a Canadian hero in this chapter. As this chapter demonstrates, the personality and identity of a celebrity acts as an ordinary attribute in a paradoxical relation to his or her extraordinary performance in fame. In political and economic contexts, the ordinary personality of a celebrity is often mediated as a national self that both raises and addresses questions of authenticity that has been lost with the rise of industrialisation. The chapter sheds particular light on the rise of Justin Bieber's celebrity on the Internet and compares online and offline gratification of national symbols in his fame. This gratification occurs on two levels that are significant for audiences and fans in a nation.

First, fans can share ideological beliefs that are reproduced in media constructions of celebrities. Here, the mode of communication among fans, as scholar James Carey argues, is ritualistic and participatory.[2] This mode of communication leads to, in Benedict Anderson's words, building an "imagined community" that is also central to the ideology of the nation. In Anderson's work on nationalism, "the nation" is constructed as an "imaginary community" because most inhabitants will never meet. It is imagined because the "members of even the smallest nation will never know most of their fellow-members, meet them, or even hear of them."[3] Hence, we invent "nations where they do not exist."[4] Given that most citizens will never meet, the narration of a nation

---

1 Amber Anna Colvin, "'Ireland's Sorrow': Michael Collins, Celebrity and Nationalist Discourse in Irish and British Newspapers," paper presented at the 2nd Global Conference: Celebrity: Exploring Critical Issues, Lisbon, 2013. See also her chapter in this volume, "'The Big Fellow Is Dead!': Michael Collins as Celebrity and Nationalist Martyr."
2 James Carey, *Communication as Culture: Essays on Media and Society* (Boston: Unwin Hyman, 1989).
3 Benedict Anderson, *Imagined Communities: Reflections on the Origin and Spread of Nationalism* (London: Verso, 1989), 6.
4 Ibid.

through texts helps to communicate central ideologies and unite the nation. It can be conversely argued that cultural industries constructing celebrities follow what scholar John Dewey called a transmission model of communication, sending messages over distance for the purpose of control. In celebrity culture, these two kinds of communication, whether for control or participation, support the formation of a community with a common economic and political system, which is central to constructing and sustaining national identity in public spaces.

Second, celebrities can offer social gratification by offering opportunities to nationwide fans to engage in celebrity worship and develop para-social relationships with celebrities in their nation. A para-social relationship can be defined as an illusion of a face-to-face relationship between a spectator and a media personality.[5] The development of para-social relationships between celebrities and fans has been historically important due to their shared identity and social functions. Scholar Chris Rojek explains that "celebrity culture is a significant institution in the normative achievement of social integration."[6] As mentioned earlier, the combination of the decline of organised religion, the democratisation of society, and the commodification of society over the last two centuries provided the foundation for the rise of celebrities.[7] Specifically, "celebrities replaced monarchy as the new symbols of recognition and belonging, and as the belief in God waned, celebrities became immortal."[8] It can be argued that the institutional power of celebrities "is very limited or nonexistent."[9] However, as Chris Rojek argues, systematic media representations and shared sense of belonging have the ability to comply with the social needs of fans and produce social cohesion. For a nation, the para-social functions of celebrities based on shared national identity help to control citizens and provide conditions for national cohesion.

The ways contemporary celebrities act as role models and strengthen national cohesion is not necessarily through classical forms of heroism and merit that were observed in the past. Elsewhere in this volume Colvin[10] offers a case

---

5　Victor Costello, *Interactivity and the "Cyber-Fan": An Exploration of Audience Involvement within the Electronic Fan Culture of the Internet* (Knoxville: The University of Tennessee, 1999) and Donal Horton and Richard Wohl, "Mass Communication and Para-Social Interaction," in *Consumption and Everyday Life*, ed. Hugh Mackay (London: Sage, 1997).
6　Chris Rojek, *Celebrity* (London: Reaktion Books, 1997), 99.
7　Ibid., 13.
8　Ibid., 14.
9　Matt Hills, *Fan Culture* (London: Routledge, 2002), 113.
10　Colvin, "'The Big Fellow Is Dead!': Michael Collins as Celebrity and Nationalist Martyr," in this volume.

study of Michael Collins to illustrate the construction of national fame as a result of his heroic qualities in leadership. Michael Collins was the Director of Intelligence for the IRA, Commander-in-Chief of the Irish Army, and negotiator of the Home Rule Treaty. As a revolutionary leader, he was popularly claimed as "The Big Fellow" on 22nd August 1922, in County Cork, Ireland. The media response to Collins' death reflected and reinforced tensions between Ireland and Britain in national discourses. His death led to a national mourning and popular identification that paved his celebrity status. The way in which Collins' national fame was constructed differs from the nationwide popularity of most celebrities these days. In this respect, Mira Moshe's work[11] is useful to consider. In *The Walk of Shame*, Mira Moshe examines Israeli Celebs Awards as a cultural site that articulates national fame and demonstrates shifts from earlier forms of heroism in the Israeli nation. In 1953 in the State of Israel, the Minister of Education initiated the bestowal of the prestigious prize to citizens that contributed merit-based talent to the development of the nation. These citizens "displayed excellent achievement, have brought about a breakthrough in their fields or have made a special contribution to Israeli society" and were awarded in the presence of the President, the Prime Minister, the Minister of Education and the Mayor of Jerusalem.[12] However, the celebration of heroic deeds declined as time progressed. Unlike nationwide celebration of achievements, the Israel Celebs Awards are offered to those who contribute to the Israeli gossip scene. Moshe shows that Israeli citizens are particularly being awarded for illegal parking, drug use, and contributions to "trash culture." These examples illustrate how classical forms of heroism and merit shifted towards being a media spectacle in acts of national cohesion.

In the contemporary celebrity culture, national fame as a media spectacle follows Daniel Boorstin's definition of celebrities. For Boorstin, celebrities are public figures that are known for "well-knowness." James Monaco further highlights that "Celebrities are, of course, well-known. But people have been well-known, more or less, for centuries."[13] Unlike heroes of the nineteenth century, celebrities now "needn't have done—needn't do—anything special. Their function isn't to act—just to be…To a large extent, celebrity has entirely

---

[11] See Moshe's chapter in this volume: "Celebrity Awards, Fan Communities and the Reconstruction of 'High' and 'Low' Cultures."

[12] Mira Moshe, "The 'Israel Celebs Awards': The Walk of Shame on the Way to Fame," in *The Walk Of Shame*, eds. Mira Moshe and Nicoleta Corbu (New York, NY: Nova Science Publishers, 2013), 77–92.

[13] James Monaco, *Celebrity: The Media as Image Makers* (New York: Dell Pub Co., 1978), 5.

superseded heroism."[14] In this view, celebrities supporting their nation need not be heroic. Crucially, they only need to be "well known" for the national values they signify.

In scholarly literature, there are three studies linking celebrities with nation which are useful to consider for an analysis of the discursive and industrial construction of celebrities in Canada. These studies are those of Joshua Gamson, Julie Rak and Mary Caudle Beltrán. For Gamson,

> [C]elebrity culture is built on major American fault lines; simultaneous pulls on the parts of producers and audiences alike to celebrate individual distinction and the equality of all, to demonstrate that success is available to all and available only to the special, to instate and to undermine a meritocratic hierarchy, to embrace and attack authority.[15]

Here, Gamson points out how celebrities function to support American national ideologies of individuality and democratic equality. While in a Canadian context, Rak expands on this to suggest that the greatness of a celebrity can be ideologically linked to the greatness of a nation. The greatness of Canadian celebrities refers to them embracing cherished national values that are often opposed to American ideologies. Hence, Beltrán considers stardom as a national force, yet one with conflicting modes of operation. These modes of operation can be observed in Canadian celebrity culture. Gamson, Rak and Beltrán's research are significant because they indicate a link between celebrities and their nations. However, the industrial and discursive process in which authenticity of celebrities is constructed by Canadian governments, media and businesses has not yet been studied in popular culture.

Popular representations show that authenticity of famous Canadian personalities is often established through intimacy with Northern nature. The representation of Northern nature in wild, vast spaces and cold climatic conditions is a recurring theme in Canadian popular culture and academic studies. In these representations, Mounties, maple leaf, ice/snow, ice hockey, Canucks, polar bears, and vast landscapes of wilderness are popular symbols of the Canadian North. In his study of celebrity endorsements of environmental conservation, Dan Brockington states that wildlife and nature is the "product of careful, calculated manipulations and editing" in cultural practices.[16] In Canada,

---

14 Ibid., 5–6.
15 Joshua Gamson, *Claims to Fame: Celebrity in Contemporary America* (Berkeley: University of California Press, 1994), 12.
16 Dan Brockington, "Powerful Environmentalisms: Conservation, Celebrity and Capitalism," *Media Culture Society* 30 (2008): 565.

selective images of Northern nature are often associated with representations of Canadian celebrities but this aspect has not been explored in academic studies yet. The selected images of Northern nature in the Canadian context serve to authenticate celebrities as well as help to authenticate the Canadian nation. As Richard Dyer states, "Authenticity is both a quality necessary to the star phenomenon to make it work, and also the quality that guarantees the authenticity of other particular values a star embodies."[17] The primordial and organic qualities of Canadian nature not only serve to authenticate a star image but also the national value that the image embodies. Since maintenance of territorial boundaries is the premise for a unifying national identity, the global reach of online fame may threaten national interests of media corporations producing and circulating Northern and other national symbols in Canada. Nevertheless, corporations often reclaim national identity of celebrities for development of national and transnational brands. The expression of a dominant national identity also helps fans to identify with online celebrities. These symbolic practices of identification in Canadian fame have not been critically investigated in media and cultural studies. This chapter will fill this gap in relation to online fame that may both challenge and restore national identity of celebrities.

2   Online Fame

Before I delve into the question of how online celebrities are constructed in relation to the nation, it is important to define who/what is an online celebrity. I define online celebrities as public personalities that become famous over the Internet as well as those who are constructed through traditional media but the Internet supports their fame in offline and online settings. There are thus two distinct types of online celebrities. First, there are online-only (or fame due to online presence) celebrities. This type of online celebrity refers to Internet users, bloggers or fans who are constructed as celebrities and who may or may not cross over to a celebrity status in traditional media. In this chapter, case studies of Justin Bieber will illustrate how online fans become celebrities. Second, there are traditional celebrities, who now have an online presence. This type of online celebrity refers to those who are already famous in print and broadcast media industries, but are also present on the Internet. Canadian star Lisa Ray's media representations can be considered as examples of reinforcing offline fame while she established an online presence.

---

17   Richard Dyer, "A Star is Born and the Construction of Authenticity," in *Stardom: Industry of Desire*, ed. Christine Gledhill (London: Routledge, 1991), 133.

The understanding of online celebrities can be informed by Kerry Ferris and Jade Alexander's work on local celebrities and roller derby. Kerry Ferris describes a local celebrity as a public figure that is "treated as famous only by and for their fan audiences."[18] Alexander, in this volume, draws on Ferris and points out the significance of local celebrities in terms of their increased accessibility. Alexander specifically maps the celebrity fan asymmetry in localised contexts that offer stronger opportunities to identify with "realness" of a talented self.[19] With the rise of social media, local celebrities, both online and offline, have opportunities to express talent in a participatory, immediate, and accessible manner. This kind of engagement contrasts past forms of interactions where fans would engage with celebrity texts in ways that were fixed in time and space. The lack of a two-way communication and active participation with celebrities led early researchers to conceptualise fans as "passive consumers and cultural dupes."[20] The impact of Internet technologies changes the production, distribution and reception of celebrity texts into participatory ones. In this respect, both fans and celebrities have greater control and can reproduce texts in variable ways to construct popularity. These changes also shift the traditional meaning of fame into one that is immediately accessible to active Internet users and can generate "overnight sensations" in certain conditions. Like local celebrities, their boundaries with fans are less distinct. Local celebrities can be online, but not all online celebrities are necessarily local. Online celebrities may differ from local celebrities in the sense that their renowned fame is not limited to fans in a closed network. Online celebrities are able to reach out to global fans in the same or increased manner observed in traditional stardom. At the same time, Internet fame is a distinct sort of celebrity, which is often temporary, fragile, and understood to be fleeting unless it gets connected to sociological conditions in the offline "star" system and maintained within existing social discourses.

To understand the sociological conditions of online fame, it is important to address the questions: In an offline setting, who can become an online celebrity? And, what are the sociological conditions of an online celebrity's production? Here, inspired from Francesco Alberoni's work, I introduce three different

---

18 Kerry O. Ferris and Scott R. Harris, "Stargazing: Celebrity, Fame, and Social Interaction," in *Contemporary Sociological Perspectives*, eds. Valerie Jenness, Irvine O'Brien and Jody O'Brien (New York and London: Routledge, 2011), 6–8.

19 See Jade Alexander, "Touching Fame: Exploring Interactional Dynamics between Local Celebrities and Fans in Sydney's Roller Derby Scene," in this volume.

20 Henry Jenkins, *Fans, Bloggers, and Gamers: Exploring Participatory Culture* (New York: New York University Press, 2006), 37.

micro and macro sociological conditions that are necessary for attaining the status and textual representation of an online celebrity. These conditions can be applied to the case studies of Canadian online celebrities presented later in this chapter. There are microsociological conditions for the construction and maintenance of an online celebrity in everyday life. These conditions are (1) Social mobility (i.e., anyone can change his or her social status based on achievement or visibility); (2) social role of a hero who may or may not have behavioural traits of serving a community but is a role model for self-achievement; and (3) emotional affinity in para-social interaction with fans. In contrast, there are macrosociological conditions required for online celebrities. These conditions are (1) large audience or large number of fans (e.g., at least over a million online users); (2) development, use, and convergence of technologies in mass communication (i.e., the Internet, telecommunications, print, broadcast media or film); and (3) broader media discourses in which online celebrity texts are produced. Once these criteria are met, traditional media often represent online celebrities within existing social discourses. These offline representations, in turn, help to stabilise their Internet fame that is otherwise fleeting in nature.

The sociological conditions for the construction of online celebrities are parallel to what Francesco Alberoni, Richard Dyer and Barry King identify as classical conditions for industrial production of stardom in traditional settings. These conditions have long existed in the Hollywood studio system. Francesco Alberoni identifies that these factors operate and determine the nature of production, distribution, and consumption of a heavily controlled star. In this context, Alberoni uses the phrase "powerless elite" to describe traditional celebrities in Hollywood. He suggests that the institutional power of celebrities is very limited or non-existent. For him, the celebrities' lack of power contrasts with their actions that "arouse a considerable [...] degree of interest."[21] However, unlike the Hollywood studio system, the cultural processes of online constructions do not necessarily conform to industrial control involved in ownership of production, distribution, and reception. For online celebrities, the conditions shift from legal and bureaucratic control to decentralised expressions of individual talent. Unlike the control of studio system and other media corporations, Internet sites are often not officially regulated in a centralised media network. In this social setting, the semiotic construction and maintenance of an online celebrity text vary in ways that make the

---

21 Francesco Alberoni, "The Powerless 'Elite': Theory and Sociological Research on the Phenomenon of the Stars," in *Sociology of Mass Communications: Selected Readings*, ed. Dennis McQuail (Harmondsworth: Penguin, 1972), 75.

text immediate and accessible to Internet users and fans, thus subject to reinvention.

Celebrities who have become famous in traditional media can also advance their fame on the Internet. In these cases, media often contrast extraordinary performances in offline settings with ordinary expressions on the Internet. The media construction of celebrities often relies on these contrasts. On the Internet, celebrities can share individual expressions through their own media text on websites. Blogs are frequently used as extratextual devices to construct and maintain a celebrity's self beyond his/her primary texts in popular media. In blogs, celebrities can post entries about his or her ordinary self and any viewer or fan can read and respond to them. Based on origin of production, there are three types of celebrity blogs. Celebrity blogs can be produced by (1) cultural industries, (2) celebrities, and (3) fans. Some cultural industries such as television stations and tabloid press create and maintain celebrity blogs where fans can interact with celebrities. These blogs can be considered part of a coherent system of promoting celebrities that carefully attracts targeted audiences.[22] In many cases, celebrities maintain their own websites or blogs.

In producing and maintaining personal websites and blogs, celebrities have opportunities to post professional and personal information about their selves. Sometimes celebrities respond to comments on fan sites as well. Such practices indicate that, as David Marshall argues, the traditional "representational gap" between the celebrity and fan is narrowing down.[23] For Marshall, the narrowing of the "representational gap" between the celebrity and the fan is driven by the emphasis on the "presentation" of self. He states that the ideology of individualism has always been a central element of consumer culture. Celebrity culture has particularly been part of "discourses of self that makes individuality concrete and real."[24] This discourse is what drives the construction and maintenance of the rhetoric of authenticity in the construction of fame. In order to establish authenticity, celebrities are usually constructed through the extratextual dimensions of private, ordinary self on the Internet.

The contrast of ordinariness on the Internet and extraordinariness of offline talent, coupled with accessibility and immediacy, is central to the construction of celebrities online. The rise of celebrities on the Internet has become ubiquitous. As scholar Rachel Derkits argues, the "decreased barrier to access

---

22 David Marshall, "New Media: New Self: The Changing Power of Celebrity," in *The Celebrity Culture Reader*, ed. David Marshall (New York: Routledge, 2006).
23 Ibid., 640.
24 Ibid., 635.

online provides an opening for new formations of celebrity."[25] In fact, journalist Rob Williams adds, "A person getting famous after being discovered online is becoming more and more common."[26] One of the online celebrities that illustrate William's report is Susan Boyle who became famous after performing on *Britain Got's Talent* and 32 million viewers saw her singing there on YouTube. Also, US-based Tila Tequila became famous for having over 1.3 million friends on MySpace.[27] Her popularity was then enhanced by being featured in traditional media such as *Stuff*, *Maxim*, *Time* and *Penthouse*. This offline fame, in turn, led to her selection as a host for Fuse TV's *Pants-Off Dance-Off* and MTV's popular reality show *A Shot at Love with Tila Tequila*. Similarly, Canadian blogger Lara Doucette became one of the Internet's most popular online celebrities. Doucette became popular as a videoblogger on *Tiki Bar TV*, one of the Internet's earliest and most popular video podcasts. Thousands of Internet fans celebrated her online performance. She became so famous that she was hired by Canada's CBC television to host their late night program *Exposure*.

The above examples show that talented individuals can gain popular recognition on the Internet. This recognition is significant for Canadian talent that often feels dominated by Hollywood in America. Once recognised on the Internet, mainstream media, including prime-time broadcast news, proclaim these artists as celebrities and represent them within existing social discourses. Online celebrities sustain their fame by subjecting themselves to the larger, on-demand gaze of millions of fans through both online and traditional media. In this way, online stars are associated with offline fame. To illustrate the creation of an online star in the Canadian context, I will look at Justin Bieber's stardom and examine how he has been represented in social discourses of the nation.

3 Justin Bieber

Justin Bieber is a Canadian teenage pop star who has become globally famous for his musical talent. Born in the Canadian town of Stratford, Bieber was a fan who received initial recognition for his online performance of songs from artists like Usher, Ne-Yo and Stevie Wonder. He attracted a worldwide recognition

---

25 Rachel Derkits, *Lukeford.com: Public Sex, Celebrity and the Internet* (Stanford: Stanford University, 2004), 27.
26 Rob William, "Maria Wouldn't Be First to Find Fame After Discovery Online," *Winnipeg Free Press* (2011), A3.
27 Lev Grossman, "Tila Tequila," *Time* (2006), accessed February 25, 2014, http://content.time.com/time/magazine/article/0,9171,1570728,00.html.

of around ten million online viewers when his mother, Pattie Mallette, posted his performances on YouTube.[28] In 2008, Bieber's online popularity grabbed attention of Atlanta-based Scooter Braun who became his manager. Soon after, Bieber obtained a recording contract with Island Records and released his first single "One Time" and album *My World* in 2009 that topped worldwide music charts. Since then, producers, media, and fans have constructed and represented Justin Bieber as a star in Canada and abroad. Bieber's fame mostly relies on his meritocratic talent. It also relies on questions of authenticity within the paradox of the "extraordinary" and "ordinary" that are specific to global and national contexts.

In general, media reports describe Bieber's extraordinariness of talent with expressions such as "teenage sensation," "superstar," and "megastar." At the same time, the reports indicate his ordinariness in two different ways. On one hand, media recognises how ordinariness complements his extraordinariness—it plays a role of familiarity with which millions of young fans can identify with Justin Bieber as an extraordinary case of merit-based talent. The extraordinary role of Bieber's ordinariness is expressed in CTV news, reporting on the promotion of his film *Never Say Never* at Toronto's Royal York Hotel: "Bieber, indeed, is a star of another era—the social networking, era, to be precise."[29] The specific reference to "social networking era" indicates an ordinary everyday life situation in which Bieber's mother simply wanted to share her son's videos with relatives by posting them on YouTube. Extraordinarily, viewers worldwide viewed these videos and recognised Justin Bieber's extraordinary talent. Justin Bieber's ordinariness thus complements his extraordinary achievements. On the other hand, Justin Bieber is known for overcoming ordinary struggles in the private space of his home, which contrasts extraordinary achievements in a public space. In this respect, media particularly emphasise Bieber's ordinariness in terms of his struggles of growing up in a poor home where his mother did two jobs and raised him as a single parent.[30] In light of this background, CTV shows how Justin Bieber is ordinary and, hence, "not perfect"[31] when he arrives at Toronto's Royal York Hotel to promote his film *Never Say Never*. The report then cites Bieber saying, "I'm a regular teenage boy [...] Lots of people

---

28   Jane Stevenson, "Justin Bieber Hits the Big Time," *Toronto Sun* (2009), accessed February 25, 2014, http://www.torontosun.com/entertainment/columnists/jane_stevenson/2009/11/16/11765871.html.

29   Constance Droganes, "'I'm Not Perfect,' Bieber Says on Return to Canada," accessed December 6, 2011, http://www.ctv.ca/CTVNews/TopStories/20110201/bieber-toronto-appearance-110201/.

30   Barry Hertz, review of *First Step 2 Forever: My Story*, by Justin Bieber, *The National Post* (2010).

31   Droganes, "'I'm Not Perfect,' Bieber Says on Return to Canada."

think I'm made by some factory machine. But I worked hard to get here [...] I'm going through different struggles and different things in my life."[32] These expressions of ordinariness contrast with Justin Bieber's extraordinariness as a talented singer. Although Bieber's authenticity may be questioned in the contrasts, it is simultaneously addressed through his ordinariness, which is central to constructing his stardom.

4   Authenticity and the Canadian Nation

Justin Bieber's stardom also relies on the contrast of ordinariness and extraordinariness in an imaginary relation to Canada. Canadian production companies and media often construct Bieber's stardom in ways that are specific to the nation. For example, a Canada.com news article, titled "Justin Bieber Fever Threatened by Cold Blast of Overexposure"[33] represents his stardom in Northern frontier conditions. The article reviews the vast number of endorsement contracts that Bieber has received and his difficulty in handling them. The article imagines this difficulty as a "cold blast of overexposure."[34] Here, the expression "cold blast" conjures up images of snowstorms and wind chills in the Northern frontier. Ethnometeorological studies on Canadian climate show how representations of cold weather are often cultural constructs, mediating national identity in a way that mythically represents endurance and strength of the North. These ordinary frontier conditions created difficulties for earlier settlers in Canada and are imagined to challenge Justin Bieber as well. In this symbolic setting, Justin Bieber's stardom is understood as an extraordinary achievement of overcoming harsh conditions in an imagined Canadian frontier. This cultural production of stardom helps to imagine the nation as strong and extraordinary.

A *Toronto Life* magazine also illustrates expressions of Canada as frontier nation in Bieber's stardom. The article, titled "Captain Canuck Goes Hollywood," reports on a Canadian film production that aims to cast Bieber as Captain Canuck.[35] According to the article, Bieber's role as Captain Canuck represents "an honest Mountie-turned-intelligence-agent [...who] gained his

---

32   Ibid.
33   Misty Harris, "Justin Bieber Fever Threatened by Cold Blast of Overexposure." *Postmedia News*, accessed December 6, 2011, http://www.canada.com/entertainment/Justin+Bieber +fever+threatened+cold+blast+overexposure/4144156/story.html.
34   Ibid.
35   Mishki Vaccaro, "Captain Canuck Goes Hollywood: Possible Movie in the Works, with Justin Bieber as the Red-Caped Crime Fighter," *Toronto Life* 28 (2011).

superpowers from an encounter with aliens while camping."[36] The symbolic association between Canuck and Mountie in the media representation of Justin Bieber can be read from the scholarly perspectives of Jason Dittmer and Soren Larsen. In their view, the word "Canuck" emerged as a national superhero in Canadian comic books and is now an informal reference to English Canadians. The imagined hero is recognised for strength, endurance, moral integrity, and less aggression.[37] These mythical traits of Canadianness are parallel to those of the Mountie in national discourses. Both the Canuck and Mountie emerge from an imagined Northern frontier. In the *Toronto Life* article, Bieber is particularly associated with "politeness" and "honesty" of a Mountie and represented as a "maple-leaf adorned superhero."[38] The imagining of his "honesty" and "politeness" underlines a moral value that has emerged from the endurance against ordinary frontier conditions in the colonial history of Canada. The official national symbols of the Mountie and maple leaf in Bieber's representation particularly signify frontier conditions of wilderness against which the nation-state was built. A rhetorical question in the *Toronto Life* article prompts us to imagine and reconstruct the frontier nation further: "But what Canadian super-talent has the gravitas, popularity charm and politeness to represent the True North's true hero? [...] the name that comes to mind is none other than Justin Bieber."[39] The mediation of Bieber's talent as "True North's true hero" shows how his authenticity is culturally constructed within national discourses of the North. It imagines harsh ordinary conditions against which Bieber's extraordinary heroism is established in Canada.

In addition to representing Justin Bieber as "True North's true hero," the *Toronto Life* article helps to imagine Bieber's fame as morally stronger than that of American stars. The article titled "Captain Canuck Goes Hollywood" suggests how Bieber may encounter imagined frontier conditions of the Wild West in Hollywood. In the film, Bieber plays the role of Captain Canuck that originally represents a Mountie. Like the Mountie represents the Northern frontier in binary relations to the Wild West, the Canuck articulates a "national identity against that of USA" and is imagined stronger and better than that of its southern counterpart.[40] The imagination is rooted in a Canadian frontier ideology whereby the North is harsher than that of the Wild West in America.

---

36 Ibid.
37 Jason Dittmer and Soren Larsen, "Captain Canuck, Audience Response, and the Project of Canadian Nationalism," *Social and Cultural Geography* 8 (2007).
38 Vaccaro, "Captain Canuck Goes Hollywood."
39 Ibid.
40 Dittmer and Larsen, "Captain Canuck."

For William Katerberg, the "North" of North America particularly acts as a site of imagining a stronger colonial power of Western conquest.[41] Here, Bieber figures as a Canuck who not only goes to Hollywood but also reminds of a collective sense of national heroism that is morally stronger than that of the US. The cinematic adaptation of the comic book and its media representation acts as an extratextual element that qualifies Bieber's stardom in Canada. Both the film and its media representation celebrate Bieber's talent as a set of Canadian qualities in relation to the US. These representations help to reclaim Bieber's Canadian national identity in Hollywood as he has migrated to the US for his music career. In the process, the media supports an authentic and sovereign representation of the Canadian nation in relation to dominant practices of the US.

The cultural imagination of Justin Bieber as Canada's national hero can be questioned from the viewpoint of other authors, such as Colvin and Yaron Girsh. In her chapter, "'The Big Fellow Is Dead!': Michael Collins as Celebrity and Nationalist Martyr," Colvin illustrates how national fame is a result of heroic qualities in revolutionary leadership in Ireland and tensions with Britain. Although the media response to Collin's death was situated in national discourses, his mortality attested merit-based talent and ways in which he challenged his life to secure his nation.[42] Yaron Girsh further shows that the notion of heroism in nation continues to be reproduced in contemporary culture. He uses the term "Biebermania" to symbolise adolescents' global craze for stars such as Justin Bieber. Such popular appeal is observed in imagining national heroes in contemporary celebrity culture. Yet, fame and heroism may not be the same kind of popularity in every nation. He expands his argument by showing how Israeli adolescents consider their parents as personal heroes and their soldiers as collective heroes as they physically fought for their country. For him, the subversion of celebrity worship in Israel is grounded in the fact that "Israeli youth has a clear leaning towards conformity and conservative values. The point of view of Israeli adolescents teaches us the way in which this culture is experienced and understood, and the way it influences youth cultures in local contexts."[43] There are some variations in the dichotomy of heroes and celebrities, especially when adolescents admire humanitarian celebrities

---

41   William Katerberg, "A Northern Vision: Frontiers and the West in the Canadian and American Imagination," *American Review of Canadian Studies* 33 (2003): 543–63.

42   Colvin, "'The Big Fellow Is Dead!': Michael Collins as Celebrity and Nationalist Martyr," in this volume.

43   Yaron Girsh, "From Beatlemania to Biebermania: Adolescent's Views of Heroes and Celebrities," *Celebrity: Exploring Critical Issues* (2013), accessed February 25, 2014, http://www

in social and political contexts of national and transnational relations. Indeed, fame carries context-based understandings. It is specific to the context in which it is produced, circulated, and received. In Canada for instance, the defence of an imagined Northern frontier does not require physical acts of protecting human rights. Rather, it is supported by media representation of Northern symbols that overlook social issues of indigenous people and global warming in the geographical north that is 60 degrees and above the latitude. The symbolic practices act as spectacular elements in national identification with and consumption of celebrities. Hence, the construction and reception of celebrities as national heroes in Canada is different from legitimate forms of heroism in other historical and culture contexts, where media spectacle and national branding had a lesser role to play.

5 National Branding in Canadian Fame

Media constructions of Justin Bieber's stardom also intersect with mundane and banal representations of the nation that contrast official symbols of the Canadian frontier. In media, representations of nation-branded products and markers help to maintain Canada as Justin Bieber's homeland. The ordinariness in consuming these products not only helps to authenticate Justin Bieber's fame but the Canadian nation as well. In a report on the press conference of *Never Say Never*, CTV describes how "Canada [is] still home for Bieber."[44] In this context, CTV cites Justin Bieber stating, "I miss Tim Hortons. I miss my friends and my family and my dog Sam."[45] For Bieber, his friends, family, and pet dog represent a situated experiences and personal sense of belonging in the ordinary settings of his home and hometown. This personal and ordinary sense of belonging is appropriated by nationwide practices of consuming Tim Hortons' coffee in Canada.

The national appropriation of situated experiences with Tim Hortons' coffee raises a question: how far does national branding of local expressions represent authenticity or "realness" of talent? A close reading of Alexander's chapter in this volume[46] prompts us to compare national and local contexts of fame

---

.inter-disciplinary.net/critical-issues/wp-content/uploads/2013/02/From-Beatlemania-to-Biebermania-Girsh.pdf.
44   Droganes, "'I'm Not Perfect,' Bieber Says on Return to Canada."
45   Ibid.
46   Alexander, "Touching Fame: Exploring Interactional Dynamics between Local Celebrities and Fans in Sydney's Roller Derby Scene."

and restore authenticity of talent representation. The comparison particularly points out the loss of self in appropriating local experiences as national symbols of Canada. In contrast with official symbols such as Mounties and the maple leaf, Tim Hortons' coffee signifies local, mundane and banal expressions of the nation in Justin Bieber's stardom. Tim Hortons figures as a national brand that symbolises coffee as a natural product, uniting citizens on a shared sense of authenticity of the land.[47] In Canada, the consumption of Tim Hortons' coffee has gained nationwide popularity due to two main reasons. First, the founder of Tim Hortons coffee was a famous Canadian hockey player, hockey itself being the most popular sport nationally. Tim Hortons' fame helps to celebrate hockey as a national pastime and, in the process, the Canadian nation. Second, the Canadian population enjoys the ordinary, mundane pleasures of consuming coffee. The marketing of the Tim Hortons franchise as a national brand represents liberation from the state regulation of popular culture.[48] The national branding of Tim Hortons coffee becomes a popular cultural marker of Canadian lifestyle. In local spaces, Canadians enjoy natural, mundane, and ordinary pleasures of everyday life as being more authentic than practices originating from the nation state. When appropriated as a national practice, these ordinary pleasures not only mediate Justin Bieber's authenticity as a real Canadian but, in the process, the Canadian nation as well. Thus, Canadian places or products within the nation offer different opportunities to imagine proximity. However, they do not necessarily offer accessibility, intimacy and pleasure with the expressions of real self. Often, they are cultural constructs that reflect and reproduce ideological boundaries that support exclusion of those who do not conform to national standards. In Canada, as seen in Justin Bieber's case, this exclusion is imagined on the basis of what America's Wild West is not or what cannot be included in the Northern frontier. Alexander observes the removal of actual physical boundaries and active engagement with fans as an expression of "realness" in celebrity culture.[49] This active engagement is significant to expressing authenticity and recognition of local celebrities. Although Alexander's research focuses on experiences with roller derby skaters in Australia, her observations point out what is being lost

---

47   Patricia Cormack, "'True Stories' of Canada: Tim Hortons and the Branding of National Identity," *Cultural Sociology* 2 (2008): 369–84.

48   Ibid.

49   Jade Alexander, "'It's Not Breeding That Kind of "I'm an Athlete" Arrogance': Roller Derby and the Construction of Local Celebrities," paper presented at the 2nd Global Conference: Celebrity: Exploring Critical Issues, Lisbon, 2013. Also, see her chapter in this volume.

in appropriating local, mundane products in Canada: active engagement and interaction with one's essence that is often mediated as a national self.

The mediation of Bieber's ordinariness in a national context is reflected in a *National Post* article as well. In reviewing his celebrity memoir *First Step 2: My Story Forever*, the article has the following claim: "From humble beginnings in some mythical land called Canada (home of 'maple syrup and Caramilk bars') to his ascent to global super-stardom, Bieber exposes himself raw to the world."[50] In this media report, maple syrup, like Tim Hortons coffee, represents ordinariness and authenticity of the raw nature of both Justin Bieber's stardom and of the Canadian land. Maple syrup is an ordinary, mundane, and natural product in Canada. As a symbol of nature, maple syrup is more authentic than the state-sanctioned emblem of the maple leaf in Canadian bureaucratic affairs. The nation branding of maple syrup becomes a symbol of nature that authenticates Justin Bieber as a Canadian and, in the process, the Canadian nation in which his stardom is constructed.

In Justin Bieber's media representations, the usage of both Tim Hortons and maple syrup reinscribes a territorially-bound identity in the very contrast it creates with state-regulated popular culture.[51] The images of these products not only help to identify and authenticate the territorially bounded Canadian nation as the home of these products but also the home or homeland of citizens. The underlying premise of associating nature and nation is the shared quest of authenticity and spiritual belonging with land that unifies a collection of people within a territory.[52] Members of the land inhabit the territory, a unit of space. As territorial space gives the impression of inhabiting home, narratives conflate home and the land, giving roots and boundaries to construct the nation as a homeland.[53] In Canada, media narratives represent natural products such as Tim Hortons coffee and maple syrup to evoke images of a homeland in which the products originate. While maple syrup naturally originates in Canada, coffee plants originate elsewhere. Yet, for media and other cultural institutions, Tim Hortons' coffee is as natural as maple syrup because the national origin of its corporation is in Canada. These products, through their origins, authenticate the territorially bounded Canadian nation as a home or homeland of its citizens.

---

50   Hertz, review of *First Step 2 Forever*.
51   Cormack, "'True Stories' of Canada: Tim Hortons and the Branding of National Identity."
52   Erin Manning, *Ephemeral Territories: Representing Nation, Home, and Identity in Canada* (Minneapolis: University of Minnesota Press, 2003).
53   Guntram Henrik Herb and David H. Kaplan, *Nested Identities: Nationalism, Territory, and Scale* (Lanham and Oxford: Rowman & Littlefield, 1999).

In this national context, the CTV report and *National Post* article[54] uses Tim Hortons and maple syrup to symbolise Justin Bieber's national identification with his homeland. The article particularly contrasts the ordinariness of Justin Bieber's Canadian home with the extraordinariness of his "global superstardom."[55] The paradox of the ordinariness of Canada as "home" and extraordinariness of "global stardom" mobilises questions of authenticity of Justin Bieber: Is he an ordinary citizen or extraordinary star? The ongoing desire to know the reality of Justin Bieber helps to create appeal and desire that is central to his stardom. At the same time, the ordinariness of home, both literally and figuratively, authenticates Justin Bieber's self. It also authenticates the territory of Canada that is both the point of departure and return for the star.

6   Conclusion

The study in this chapter illustrated that both traditional and online media represent and sustain online Canadian celebrities within national discourses. The national identity of online celebrities can be expressed in contrasting ways. At times, media producers and Internet users associate online celebrities with official symbols of the nation. In particular, this chapter shows how Justin Bieber's stardom is articulated in relation to official national symbols such as the Canadian flag, maple leaf, and Mounties. At other times, online celebrities are associated with banal and mundane products and practices that are not sanctioned by the nation-state yet mark "Canadianness" in everyday life. In representations of online celebrities, the North, Captain Canuck, maple syrup, and Tim Hortons often figure and mark "Canadianness." Some of these markers and products contrast with official symbols as they signify everyday life pleasures of consumption and freedom from the state bureaucracy. Yet, they overlap with official symbols as they signify Canadian myths that largely associate the nation with the dominance of an English Canadian identity in an imagined Northern frontier.

For Canadian cultural institutions, the significance of using national symbols and markers online lies in reclaiming the national identity of celebrities. This act of reclaiming is significant when the Internet allows fame to transcend territorial boundaries, for example when celebrities such as Justin Bieber receive contracts in Hollywood after gaining initial online fame. In the historical and political context of Canadian identity crisis, the construction

---

54   Hertz, review of *First Step 2 Forever*.
55   Ibid.

and maintenance of Canadian national symbols might be challenging or less important on the Internet. The maintenance of territorial boundaries, the premise for a unifying national identity,[56] may threaten the nationality of an online celebrity. Nevertheless, media and audiences are often able to reclaim Canadian national identity of global celebrities with the help of local symbols that characterise territorial boundaries of the nation.

Indeed, online media discourses engage with those of the nation in offline, territorial settings. In these ways, media producers and audiences are able to mitigate or negotiate what might be perceived as global-national tensions in maintaining online territorial integrity. For example, I have shown that although Justin Bieber is a global star, Canadian media imagine and represent him in relation to urban experiences of his hometown Stratford and national markers of Canada. This Canadian representation occurs despite the fact that most of the time Justin Bieber does not live in Canada. Media corporations such as CTV and *National Post* produce and represent Justin Bieber as Canadian using offline symbols and myths of the nation. The material production of these texts takes place in both online and offline versions of their reports. From a material and symbolic perspective, then, the texts of online celebrities intersect with offline texts of the nation. These expressions of national identity are common with purely offline stardom, but in the online cases, the expressions are further supported by the participation of fans.

Bibliography

Alberoni, Fransesco. "The Powerless 'Elite': Theory and Sociological Research on the Phenomenon of the Stars." In *Sociology of Mass Communications: Selected Readings*, edited by Dennis McQuail, 75–98. Harmondsworth: Penguin, 1972.

Beltrán, Mary Caudle. *Bronze Seduction: The Shaping of Latina Stardom in Hollywood Film and Star Publicity*. Austin: The University of Texas, 2002.

Bieber, Justin. *Justin Bieber: First Step 2 Forever: My Story*. New York: HarperCollins Publishers, 2010.

Boorstin, Daniel. *The Image: A Guide to Pseudo-Events in America*. New York: Athenaneum, 1962.

Cormack, Patricia. "'True Stories' of Canada: Tim Hortons and the Branding of National Identity." *Cultural Sociology* 2 (2008): 369–84.

Chu, Jon M. *Justin Bieber: Never Say Never*. USA, 2011.

Dewey, John. *Democracy and Education*. New York: MacMillan, 1916.

---

56   Herb and Kaplan, *Nested Identities*.

Dittmer, Jason, and Soren Larsen. "Captain Canuck, Audience Response, and the Project of Canadian Nationalism." *Social and Cultural Geography* 8 (2007): 736–53.

Droganes, Constance. "'I'm Not Perfect,' Bieber Says on Return to Canada." Bell Media 2011. Accessed December 6, 2011. http://www.ctv.ca/CTVNews/TopStories/20110201/bieber-toronto-appearance-110201/.

Dyer, Richard. *Stars*. Bury St. Edmunds: St. Edmundsbury Press, 1998.

Osborne, Brian. "From Native Pines to Diasporic Geese: Placing Culture, Setting Our Sites, Locating Identity in a Transnational Canada." *Canadian Journal of Communication* 31 (2006): 147–75.

Eriksen, Thomas Hylland. "Nationalism and the Internet." *Nations and Nationalism* 13 (2007): 1–17.

Harris, Misty. "Justin Bieber Fever Threatened by Cold Blast of Overexposure." *Postmedia News*. Accessed December 6, 2011. http://www.canada.com/entertainment/Justin+Bieber+fever+threatened+cold+blast+overexposure/4144156/story.html.

Herb, Guntram Henrik, and David H. Kaplan. *Nested Identities: Nationalism, Territory, and Scale*. Lanham and Oxford: Rowman & Littlefield, 2007.

Hertz, Barry. Review of *Justin Bieber: First Step 2 Forever: My Story*, by Justin Bieber. *The National Post*, 14 October, 2010.

Katerberg, William. "A Northern Vision: Frontiers and the West in the Canadian and American Imagination." *American Review of Canadian Studies* 33 (2003): 543–63.

Kaufmann, Eric, and Oliver Zimmer. "In Search of the Authentic Nation: Landscape and National Identity in Canada and Switzerland." *Nations and Nationalism* 4 (1998): 483–510.

King, Barry. "Articulating Stardom." In *Stardom: Industry of Desire*, edited by C. Gledhill, 167–82. London: Routledge, 1991.

Manning, Erin. "I Am Canadian." *Identity, Territory and the Canadian National Land. Theory & Event* 4 (2000). Accessed August 25, 2013. http://muse.jhu.edu/journals/theory_and_event/v004/4.4manning.html.

Manning, Erin. *Ephemeral Territories: Representing Nation, Home, and Identity in Canada*. Minneapolis: University of Minnesota Press, 2003.

MTV. "MTV: Justin Bieber Artist Profile." Accessed December 6, 2011. http://www.mtv.com/music/artist/bieber_justin/artist.jhtml#biographyEnd.

Rak, Julie. "Canadian Idols? CBC's *The Greatest Canadians* as Celebrity History." In *Programming Reality: Perspectives on English-Canadian Television*, edited by Druick Zoe, 51–68. Waterloo, Ontario: Wilfrid Laurier University Press, 2008.

Stevenson, Jane. "Justin Bieber Hits the Big Time." *Toronto Sun*, 16 November 2009.

Vaccaro, Mishki. "Captain Canuck Goes Hollywood: Possible Movie in the Works, with Justin Bieber as the Red-Caped Crime Fighter." *Toronto Life*, 28 January, 2011.

CHAPTER 3

Literary Celebrity, Politics and the Nobel Prize: The Nobel Lecture as an Authorial Self-Fashioning Platform

Sandra Mayer

Abstract

Regardless of Roland Barthes' forcefully proclaimed "death of the author," authorial agency has remained a controversially discussed concept in contemporary critical debate, and the sphere of literary production continues to exploit the reputational capital and star potential of literary brand names. The proliferation and intense media coverage of literary prizes, in particular, attest to the firm ties between cultural and economic capital. By taking a close look at the lectures delivered by two successive Nobel Laureates, this chapter seeks to explore the ways in which the publicity generated by high-profile literary prizes provides authors with a powerful platform for self-fashioning. Both the Austrian writer Elfriede Jelinek and the British dramatist Harold Pinter, respective winners of the Nobel Prize in Literature in 2004 and 2005, have a career history as astute left-wing intellectuals, political activists, and cultural critics, sharing a larger-than-life public image that has been shaped by an intricate interplay of art and politics. A comparative analysis of their Nobel lectures aims at highlighting the multi-medial forms and strategies of authorial self-representation and thus ultimately touches upon some of the core debates of celebrity studies, such as the dichotomy of public vs. private self, negotiations of absence and presence, and the political power of celebrity.

When the Nobel Laureate in Literature of 2004, Elfriede Jelinek, delivered her Nobel Lecture on 7 December 2004, it was the Austrian novelist and playwright's carefully choreographed virtual presence as an oversized digital image that filled three projection screens at the Swedish Academy's Stockholm Börssalen. Pleading her agoraphobia and pathological horror of large crowds in practically each of her public statements on her Nobel award,[1] Jelinek had

---

1 Talking to a Swedish broadcaster immediately after the official announcement of her Nobel Prize success in October 2004, Jelinek was adamant about her decision not to attend the

opted for a 40-minute video lecture, recorded in the highly private environment of her Vienna family home, which both subverted and reconciled notions of presence and absence, public visibility and withdrawal. Indeed, Jelinek's speech, monotonously delivered in front of a music stand as an intimately soft-spoken conversation with herself, contained an intensely personal assessment of her position as an alienated, "sidelined" artist both striving for, and longing to, escape the isolation and remoteness experienced by the reclusive writer, thus underlining the author's active role in the performative construction of her protean public image oscillating between narcissism and self-deprecation, exhibitionism and shyness.

Precisely twelve months later, the illustrious audience gathered at the same venue was confronted with a similar spectacle of elaborately staged and mediated authorial presence when his frail health had prevented that year's Literature Nobel Laureate, the British playwright and poet Harold Pinter, from travelling to Stockholm and launching his scathing attack on the emptiness of political rhetoric and the dictatorial self-righteousness of US foreign policy in person. As theatre critic and Pinter biographer Michael Billington noted in *The Guardian*, there was indeed something "oddly Beckettian" about the video-taped and broadcast image of the author sitting in a wheelchair, with a plaid blanket thrown over his knees. Pinter delivered his fervent speech on "Art, Truth and Politics" in a strained and raspy voice before a life-sized faded portrait shot of his younger and more physically robust self.[2] Intently fixing his unwavering stare on the camera and peppering his speech with the strategically placed moments of portentous silence that have come to be known in the discourse of literary criticism as "Pinter pauses," the former stage actor and director dextrously employed "every weapon in his theatrical technique to reinforce his message."[3]

Both Jelinek and Pinter have been known as astute left-wing intellectuals, political activists, and cultural critics, sharing a larger-than-life public image that has been shaped by an intricate interplay of art and politics. Albeit for different reasons, their conspicuous absences at the award ceremonies in

---

Stockholm award ceremony in person: "I would gladly do it but I am suffering from social phobia. I cannot manage being in a crowd of people. I cannot stand public attention, I just can't." Anders Lindqvist, "Interview with Elfriede Jelinek, October 2004," *Nobelprize.org*, accessed September 5, 2012, http://www.nobelprize.org/nobel_prizes/literature/laureates/2004/jelinek-interview_text.html.

2 Michael Billington, "Passionate Pinter's Devastating Assault on US Foreign Policy," *The Guardian*, December 8, 2005, accessed September 14, 2012, http://www.guardian.co.uk/uk/2005/dec/08/books.nobelprize.

3 Ibid.

Stockholm and their video-taped speeches present minutely scripted media performances in which the "virtual presence" of the author adds poignancy to his/her discursive self-projection, be it in the form of Pinter's inflammatory political propaganda or Jelinek's programmatic outline of her self-image as a writer and her aesthetics. Not surprisingly, their multi-medial strategies of authorial self-representation attracted a flurry of media attention as they cunningly exploited the ambiguous interplay of the literary celebrity's public and private selves.

The voyeuristic gaze of the public is invariably obsessed with the desire to recover the individual's "true" and "authentic" self behind the mask of the renowned public persona, and, paradoxically, the authorial pose of absence, elusiveness, and inaccessibility thus only serves to increase the author's ubiquity and media exposure.[4] In fact, the author's conscious disengagement from conventional modes of public self-representation (as famously practised by such iconic author recluses as J.D. Salinger or Thomas Pynchon) contributes to the mythical dimensions of literary stardom as it becomes a focal point of critical attention that is frequently interpreted as "either a heroic gesture or a publicity stunt."[5] Without doubt, Jelinek has been a highly visible presence in the public sphere as a readily accessible and quotable interviewee and one of the most frequently photographed German-language women writers, whose eccentric hairdo and heavy make-up underline her ironic commentary on traditional gender roles. At the same time, the author's skilful media self-fashioning has been perceived to be at odds with her carefully cultivated image of an enigmatic literary recluse dragged into the limelight against her will and has repeatedly drawn facetious comments in the German-language press.[6] Just like Oscar Wilde, whose celebrity persona is shown to be a collaborative creation by author and audience in Anna Fomichenko's contribution to this volume,[7] Elfriede Jelinek must be regarded an active co-author of her public image. A professed Wilde enthusiast herself who has repeatedly identified the

---

4 Joe Moran, *Star Authors: Literary Celebrity in America* (London: Pluto Press, 2000), 63.
5 Ibid., 66.
6 For instance, Katharina Rutschky in *Die Welt* thus comments on Jelinek's self-contradictory media representations: "Like a timid fawn she rushes from one interview to the next. Is she an anti-fascist and radical feminist or rather something above or below that? At any rate, she looks like an UFA film star of the 1930s." [All translations from the German are the author's]. Katharina Rutschky, "Einstürzende Dramenkostüme," *Die Welt*, October 15, 2004, accessed January 2, 2013, http://www.welt.de/print-welt/article346266/Einstuerzende-Damenkostueme.html.
7 See Anna Fomichenko, "Oscar Wilde's Long Afterlife: Victorian Celebrity and Its Transformations in Modern Culture," in this volume.

Irish author as part of her literary ancestry,[8] Jelinek has followed in Wildean footsteps, persistently generating public attention by resisting any attempts at clear-cut and finite categorisation and thus perpetually renewing audience interest.

As the German literary critic Ursula März notes in *Die Zeit*, Jelinek's systematically conducted shift from physical to virtual public presence, her gradual transformation into a subject accessible only through an elaborately constructed image, is powerfully demonstrated by the auratic pre-eminence of the author's appearance as a larger-than-life video projection that is remote and within easy reach, aloof and intimate at the same time.[9] In her essay on the "intrinsic celebrificatory power" of the Nobel Prize in Literature as a specifically European institution of cultural consecration, Rebecca Braun observes that while Jelinek ostensibly seeks to opt out of literary celebrity industry, she

> is consolidating her own image as a trenchant cultural critic, as well as unquestionably furthering the European tradition of the author as a public moral instructor. Thus, even as she buys out of literary celebrity as a media process underpinned by commodity fetishism, she cannot help but buy back into the particular form of creator fetishism that underpins its European manifestation.[10]

As heavily publicised and glamorous media events that have become a hallmark of what James F. English refers to as the "'economy of spectacle'" in modern cultural life,[11] high-profile literary awards such as the Nobel Prize in Literature undoubtedly provide authors with a powerful platform of self-fashioning. What is more, they both create and readily exploit the reputational capital and star potential of literary brand names, which freely circulate as

---

8   Sharing Wilde's obsession with rhetoric, style and surface, Jelinek is the author of two widely noted, eccentric adaptations of Wilde's *The Importance of Being Earnest* and *An Ideal Husband*, which both premièred in Vienna's Akademietheater in 2005 and 2011 respectively.

9   Ursula März, "Elfriede und Elfriede," *Zeit Online*, December 16, 2004, accessed January 2, 2013, http://www.zeit.de/2004/52/KA-LIT_LEBEN52.

10 Rebecca Braun, "Fetishising Intellectual Achievement: The Nobel Prize and European Literary Celebrity," *Celebrity Studies* 2, no. 3 (2011): 330.

11 James F. English, *The Economy of Prestige: Prizes, Awards and the Circulation of Cultural Value* (Cambridge: Harvard University Press, 2005), 34.

"promotional signs"[12] in an increasingly commodified "'meet-the-author' culture" as a regular feature of literary festivals, public readings, TV talk shows, and academic conferences.[13] Notably, English attributes the "cultural frenzy" of the contemporary prize culture to "the fact that [prizes] are the single best instrument for negotiating transactions between cultural and economic, cultural and social, or cultural and political capital—which is to say that they are our most effective institutional agents of *capital intraconversion*."[14] Thus, highlighting the firm ties between cultural, economic, social, and political capital, literary honours and award ceremonies function as important forms of "institutionalized consecration"[15] that crucially affect sales figures, publishing deals, artistic reputations, and authorial prestige.

Without doubt, the Nobel Prize in Literature, awarded by the Swedish Academy in a highly ritualised and archaic procedure,[16] counts as the most prestigious, financially rewarding, and yet heavily contested of cultural prizes, comparable, as Burton Feldman argues, to a "knighthood [...] of a new and unusual kind, perhaps the only true aristocracy in our democratic, levelling age."[17] As English notes, the award has become an instrument "well suited to achieving cultural objectives along three main axes: social, institutional, and ideological."[18] In its social dimension, the prize is part of the "cultural game" and thus presents a glamorous highlight in the annual calendar of cultural events and festivals that brings together a whole range of important stakeholders in the field of culture, such as artists, critics, and sponsors. On an institutional level, literary Nobel honours represent a "claim to authority" in the production of cultural value, exercising "control over the cultural economy, over the distribution of esteem and reward on a particular cultural field"; the prize gives

---

12 Andrew Wernick, "Authorship and the Supplement of Promotion," in *What Is an Author?*, eds. Maurice Biriotti and Nicola Miller (Manchester: Manchester University Press, 1993), 90.
13 Richard Todd, *Consuming Fictions: The Booker Prize and Fiction in Britain Today* (London: Bloomsbury, 1996), 100.
14 English, *Economy of Prestige*, 18 and 10.
15 Pierre Bourdieu, "The Field of Cultural Production, Or: The Economic World Reversed," *Poetics* 12 (1983): 332.
16 According to Burton Feldman, the Nobel award ceremony appears as "a vestige of the vanished aristocratic past when princes rewarded artists or political favourites. The Nobel rite is performed for a modernity nostalgic for such older and vanishing glories." Burton Feldman, *The Nobel Prize: A History of Genius, Controversy and Prestige* (New York: Arcade, 2000), 10.
17 Ibid., 1.
18 English, *Economy of Prestige*, 50.

power to the functionaries involved in the administration of the prize and thus promotes the "bureaucratization of art."[19] Finally, from an ideological point of view, the prize puts to a test the notion of art as an autonomous realm: "Precisely because this notion of art and of artistic value requires continual acts of collective make-believe to sustain it, there is a need for events which foster certain kinds of collective cultural (mis)recognition."[20] In any case, the award's *en-Nobeling* quality as a major catalyst in the production and consolidation of literary stardom—what Feldman calls the "monumentalizing process"[21]— finds striking expression in the way the defining epithet "Nobel Prize-winning" persistently makes catchy media headlines and has come to signify well-nigh universal renown and cultural authority as an ostensibly reliable marker of artistic merit and distinction.[22]

While Harold Pinter could already boast a considerable degree of literary celebrity as an internationally acclaimed playwright, the widespread media coverage of Elfriede Jelinek's Nobel honours substantially increased the author's international profile and was subsequently vigorously exploited by translators, publishers, and the book trade in an attempt to maximise the profits from the sale and production of her works.[23] Specifically, Jelinek's four novels translated into English by then (*The Piano Teacher, Women as Lovers, Wonderful Wonderful Times, Lust*), while not exactly bestsellers in the literary marketplace, experienced a dramatic rise in sales[24] despite a marked media tendency to pigeonhole her as an obscure and notoriously difficult avant-garde writer. Indeed, British and US-American reactions frequently betrayed a palpable sense of disappointment and puzzled irritation over the choice of a barely known, virtually untranslatable Austrian feminist writer instead of an easily marketable literary heavyweight, as evidenced by a *Daily Telegraph* article quoting a disgruntled British literary agent at the Frankfurt Book Fair: "'I have just come from a lunch with four top British publishers and not one of

---

19   Ibid., 51 and 52.
20   Ibid., 52–3.
21   Feldman, *The Nobel Prize*, 18.
22   Ibid., 1. John Street, "'Showbusiness of a Serious Kind': A Cultural Politics of the Arts Prize," *Media, Culture & Society* 27, no. 6 (2005): 835.
23   Pia Janke, "Vorwort," in *Literaturnobelpreis Elfriede Jelinek*, eds. Pia Janke et al. (Vienna: Praesens, 2005), 9–10.
24   As reported in *The New York Times*, Jelinek's novel *The Piano Teacher* made a sensationally steep climb from no. 1,163,804 to No. 9 on Amazon's online sales rankings just after the Nobel announcement. Ben Sisario, "A Post-Nobel Roller Coaster," *The New York Times*, October 11, 2004, accessed January 2, 2013, http://www.nytimes.com/2004/10/11/arts/11arts.html?_r=0.

us had heard of her [Jelinek]. The Swedes are so perverse that the prize doesn't count for much any longer.'"[25] As if to prove the journalist's point that Jelinek was hardly a familiar name "outside the German-speaking world," it is consistently misspelled as "Jelenik."[26]

Both chastised and praised for pedestalising lesser known literary talent, the Nobel Prize in Literature has also faced repeated criticism for allegedly being an ideologically inflected "artist-as-humanitarian award"[27] that frequently makes a point of honouring minority literatures and/or politically active and outspoken writers, such as Jean-Paul Sartre, Aleksandr Solzhenitsyn, Wole Soyinka, Nadine Gordimer, or J.M. Coetzee. While the Swedish Academy keeps refuting charges of politically motivated decisions, Kjell Espmark, former Chairman of the Nobel Committee, acknowledges "the political aspect of any international literary prize" and points out that the actual impact and potential ideological instrumentalisation of the Academy decision can neither be predicted nor controlled.[28]

For most commentators, the choices of both Pinter and Jelinek appear reflective of "a preference for literature with a political echo."[29] Revered and reviled for her scathing criticism of modern capitalist, chauvinist, xenophobic society and Austria's post-fascist "cultural amnesia,"[30] Jelinek is described by the *Guardian* correspondent Joëlle Stolz as "an intransigent, uncompromising novelist and playwright who casts a pitiless eye on her native Austria," and is thus perceived as part of a specifically Austrian tradition of such relentless language critics as Karl Kraus and Thomas Bernhard.[31] Indeed, a traditional moralist at heart, whose lamentation of the human condition is voiced with well-nigh Cassandrian insight,[32] Elfriede Jelinek in her writing seeks to unmask

---

25 Nigel Reynolds, "Controversial Feminist Writer Wins Nobel Prize," *The Telegraph*, October 8, 2004, accessed January 2, 2013, http://www.telegraph.co.uk/news/worldnews/europe/germany/1473689/Controversial-feminist-writer-wins-Nobel-Prize.html.

26 Ibid.

27 English, *Economy of Prestige*, 58.

28 Kjell Espmark, "The Nobel Prize in Literature," *Nobelprize.org*, accessed September 26, 2012, http://www.nobelprize.org/nobel_prizes/literature/articles/espmark/.

29 Terence Neilan, "Fiery Austrian Writer Wins Nobel Prize for Literature," *The New York Times*, October 7, 2004, accessed January 2, 2013, http://www.nytimes.com/2004/10/07/books/07CND-NOBE.html?_r=0.

30 Matthias Konzett, *The Rhetoric of National Dissent in Thomas Bernhard, Peter Handke and Elfriede Jelinek* (Rochester: Camden House, 2000), 108.

31 Joëlle Stolz, "Austria, I Hate You," *The Guardian*, October 22, 2004, accessed August 24, 2010, http://www.guardian.co.uk/theguardian/2004/oct/22/guardianweekly.guardianweekly1.

32 Hans-Gert Roloff, "Vorwürfe mache ich ja immer, das ist mein Markenzeichen. Die Jelinek und ihr Theater" in *Positionen der Jelinek-Forschung: Beiträge zur Polnisch-Deutschen*

and subvert the authoritarian power structures of the bourgeois establishment. In those of her works classified as "anti-*Heimat* literature,"[33] she has consistently laid bare the remnants of a deeply ingrained fascist mindset at the core of Austrian cultural identity, which tended to be conveniently glossed over in the context of a post-World War II programme of "pseudo-normalization."[34] Aiding the consolidation of an economically prosperous model republic with a picture-postcard image "of a tourist and cultural sanctuary located in the heart of Europe,"[35] this reconstruction policy of social harmonisation and political consensus successfully obstructed any serious confrontation with Austria's National Socialist past. Moreover, it seems to have resulted in what Jelinek describes as the "collective will to infinite blamelessness."[36]

Not surprisingly, therefore, the Swedish Academy decision in favour of Jelinek unleashed an exceptional degree of polarisation, with international media responses ranging from the grudgingly appreciative to the contemptuously dismissive and personally insulting. In particular, it was her long-standing Austrian Communist party membership and her fierce anti-right-wing radicalism that became the focus of national and international media attention, as most poignantly revealed by Stephen Schwartz's vitriolic diatribe in the US neo-conservative *Weekly Standard*, in which Jelinek is savagely reviled as a "sensationalist, Communist, and anti-American hack." Her work is stridently dismissed as "verg[ing] on gross pornography," and her Nobel Prize is thought to "prove[...] that Arnold Schwarzenegger is the only decent thing to come out of that Alpine land in the last two decades." To Schwartz, the Nobel recognition of "an Austrian ogress" provides unmistakable proof of the fact that the award "each year increasingly diminishes in moral, if not in financial worth" as the Swedish Academy doggedly sticks to its "habit of awarding the Nobel Prize for

---

    Elfriede Jelinek-Konferenz Olsztyn 2005, eds. Claus Zittel and Marian Holona (Bern: Peter Lang, 2008), 156.

33   Monika Szczepaniak, "*Kennen Sie Dieses SCHÖNE Land*? Elfriede Jelineks Anti-Idyllen," in *Positionen der Jelinek-Forschung: Beiträge zur Polnisch-Deutschen Elfriede Jelinek-Konferenz Olsztyn 2005*, eds. Claus Zittel and Marian Holona (Bern: Peter Lang, 2008), 222.

34   Edna Epelbaum, "The Stage as Accomplice: Elfriede Jelinek's Politics of the *Burgtheater*," in *Elfriede Jelinek: Writing Woman, Nation, and Identity: A Critical Anthology*, eds. Matthias Piccolruaz Konzett and Margarete Lamb-Faffelberger (Madison: Fairleigh Dickinson University Press, 2007), 116.

35   Matthias Piccolruaz Konzett, "Preface: The Many Faces of Elfriede Jelinek," in *Elfriede Jelinek: Writing Woman, Nation, and Identity: A Critical Anthology*, eds. Matthias Piccolruaz Konzett and Margarete Lamb-Faffelberger (Madison: Fairleigh Dickinson University Press, 2007), 8.

36   Elfriede Jelinek, "Wir Herren der Toten," in *O Österreich!*, ed. Heinz Arnold Ludwig (Göttingen: Wallstein, 1995), 8.

Literature to an unknown, undistinguished, leftist fanatic." According to Schwartz, this category of writers also comprises "the scolding lefty turned Nazi-nostalgic Gunter Grass," the "repellent Dario Fo," the "Castro-lover" Gabriel Garcia Marquez, or the "Stalinist secret police agent" Pablo Neruda: "if America will hate it, then it rates with the Swedes."[37]

Similarly, the responses triggered by the news of Harold Pinter's Nobel award suggest that in the public eye the author's art and relentless political activism had become inseparably intertwined, forging a media image of "the angry playwright"—the artist as ferocious agitator and uncompromising dissector of domestic and world politics.[38] David Hare, in a warm personal tribute, praises his friend and fellow playwright as "the most prominent spokesperson in this country for those who are the hapless victims of belligerence and oppression,"[39] while broadcaster Melvyn Bragg, with a mildly patronising note of condescension, commends the "other side of Pinter we love so much: his sabre-toothed tiger comments on, and involvement in, contemporary politics."[40] Even Pinter himself did not deny the possibility that his public profile as a harshly critical left-wing intellectual and human rights campaigner could have influenced the Nobel Committee's decision, since, as he told *The Guardian* immediately after the Nobel announcement in October 2005, "my political engagement is very much part of my work."[41]

Just as the Nobel Prize in Literature itself has triggered controversy over its inherently political dimension as a "peace prize in literary disguise,"[42] the Nobel award ceremonies and public lectures regularly bear striking testimony to the discursive power of celebrity status. As P. David Marshall has shown in his influential study on *Celebrity and Power*, "within society, the celebrity is a

---

37 All quotes in this paragraph are from Stephen Schwartz, "Oops ... They Did It Again: The Nobel Prize for Literature goes to Elfriede Jelinek: Sensationalist, Communist, and Anti-American Hack," *The Weekly Standard*, October 8, 2004, accessed January 2, 2013, http://www.weeklystandard.com/Content/Public/Articles/000/000/004/746mjtym.asp.

38 Harry Derbyshire, "Pinter as Celebrity," in *The Cambridge Companion to Harold Pinter*, ed. Peter Raby (Cambridge: Cambridge University Press, 2009), 266.

39 David Hare, "'In Pinter You Find Expressed the Great Struggle of the 20th Century,'" *The Guardian* G2, October 14, 2005, 8.

40 Melvyn Bragg, "Nobel Art of Harold Pinter," *The Daily Mirror*, October 14, 2005, accessed September 25, 2012, http://www.mirror.co.uk/3am/celebrity-news/nobel-art-of-harold-pinter-561240.

41 Harold Pinter, "'They Said You've a Call from the Nobel Committee. I Said, Why?'" *The Guardian*, October 14, 2005, accessed September 14, 2012, http://www.guardian.co.uk/uk/2005/oct/14/books.nobelprize.

42 Feldman, *Nobel Prize*, 56.

voice above others, a voice that is channeled into the media systems as being legitimately significant,"[43] which has repeatedly motivated and enabled a considerable number of Literature Nobel Laureates to take advantage of their heightened media exposure and prominent public position in order to make rousing political statements that draw attention to specific causes. In fact, what unites (entertainment) celebrities and politicians is their "representation of affective power,"[44] their "capacity [...] to embody the collective in the individual, which identifies their cultural signs as powerful,"[45] as Marshall argues:

> First, the political leader, like the celebrity, is produced as a commodity. Second, the symbolic content of the political leader as commodity arises primarily from the similar groundwork of common cultural sentiments. Entertainment celebrities, like political leaders, work to establish a form of cultural hegemony. [...] Popularity, or the temporal establishment of a connection to a significant configuration of cultural symbols, is essential for both the politician and the celebrity.[46]

When William Butler Yeats was awarded the prize in 1923, he was determined to put himself into the service of the newly created Irish Free State and proceeded to connect art and politics in his Nobel lecture on "The Irish Dramatic Movement," in which he made a point of sketching out the history and formation of an Irish national theatre and which subsequently became a canonical text of Irish literary history.[47] Described by Per Hallström, Chairman of the Swedish Academy's Nobel Committee, as "the interpreter of his country, a country that had long waited for someone to bestow on it a voice,"[48] Yeats, as recently appointed Senator for the Irish Free State, had undergone a remarkable transformation from nationalist revolutionary to respectable elder statesman. In a letter to Edmund Gosse he acknowledged the political implications of the Nobel Prize:

---

43   P. David Marshall, *Celebrity and Power: Fame in Contemporary Culture* (Minneapolis: University of Minnesota Press, 1997), x.
44   Ibid., 185.
45   Ibid., 241.
46   Ibid.
47   See William Butler Yeats, "The Bounty of Sweden," in *Autobiographies* (London: Macmillan & Co., 1956), 531–72.
48   Per Hallström, "Award Ceremony Speech 10 December 1923," *Nobelprize.org*, accessed February 27, 2013, http://www.nobelprize.org/nobel_prizes/literature/laureates/1923/press.html.

> I am grateful too because I have a better chance of being listened to in Dublin than ever before. Of course I know quite well that this honour is not given to me as an individual but as a representative of a literary movement and of a nation and I am glad to have it so.[49]

Yeats undoubtedly had an acute sense of the political power of celebrity status, which, as Amber Anna Colvin demonstrates in her chapter on the posthumous media reception of Michael Collins, neatly served the agendas of Irish nationalist discourse. However, not all Irish Nobel Prize-winners were prepared to render their institutional recognition and international media attention serviceable to the propagandistic purposes of Irish nationalism. While Yeats deliberately styled himself as one of the foundational figures and prime representatives of a specifically Irish literary movement that attested to the country's national and cultural independence, his fellow-Dubliner Bernard Shaw was deeply sceptical of both political instrumentalisation and literary stardom, which he feared might result in creative disempowerment and loss of provocative edge. When his Nobel success was announced on 12 November 1926, his first impulse was to reject both the award and £7,000 prize money, as he resented "the spectacle of other nations begging prizes from a Swedish dynamite millionaire for their art and literature and science."[50] With characteristically biting humour, he asked the Permanent Secretary of the Royal Swedish Academy to "confer on me the additional and final honour of classing my works [...] *hors concours*":

> For the award I have nothing but my best thanks. But after the most careful consideration I cannot persuade myself to accept the money. My readers and audiences provide me with more than sufficient money for my needs; and as to my renown it is greater than is good for my spiritual health. Under these circumstances the money is a lifebelt thrown to a swimmer who has already reached the shore in safety.[51]

Eventually, he grudgingly accepted the honour and used the monetary reward for the creation of an Anglo-Swedish Literary Foundation, one of whose

---

49 William Butler Yeats, *The Letters of William Butler Yeats*, ed. Allan Wade (London: Rupert Hart-Davis, 1954), 701.
50 Bernard Shaw, *Collected Letters 1926–1950*, ed. Dan H. Laurence (London: Max Reinhardt, 1988), 52.
51 Ibid., 33–4.

primary objectives was to promote the translation of Swedish literature into English. Just like Samuel Beckett more than forty years later, he refused to travel to Stockholm to deliver a Nobel lecture and, in his absence, his medal and diploma were presented to the British Ambassador in Sweden.[52]

Quite in contrast, Harold Pinter showed no reluctance to make extensive use of the glaring media spotlight turned on him in the wake of his Nobel honours and his programmatically entitled Nobel lecture "Art, Truth and Politics" forcefully attests to the writer's fully accomplished politicisation ever since the early 1980s and his ensuing self-understanding as a socially responsible and politically conscious "citizen-playwright" who would sternly point his finger at the ills of contemporary politics and society.[53] A long-standing supporter of Amnesty International, the Campaign for Nuclear Disarmament, Arts for Nicaragua, and the Index on Censorship, Pinter, together with his wife Antonia Fraser, in 1988 founded the June 20 Group, which was intended as a force against Thatcherite Conservatism but was frequently derided in the English press as a circle of "champagne radicals."[54] Referring to the early stages of his career, when he steadfastly rejected the idea of a *littérature engagée* that expected the writer to embrace a particular socio-political concern with prophetic zeal, Pinter starts off by trying to forge a distinction between his twin roles as author and politically committed citizen, who has the moral obligation to strive towards a clear-cut division between truth and falsehood: "As a citizen I must ask: What is true? What is false?"[55] However, in view of Pinter's overtly political later work, including his plays *One for the Road* (1984) and *Mountain Language* (1989) or *War*, his 2003 volume of poetry on the Iraq War, it seems that such a categorical separation between artist and citizen can hardly be maintained. Pinter's much-quoted dismissive assessment of 1960s political theatre thus acquires highly ironic significance:

> There is certainly a good deal of prophecy indulged in by playwrights these days, in their plays and out of them. Warnings, sermons, admonitions, ideological exhortations, moral judgements, defined problems

---

52 Michael Holroyd, *Bernard Shaw, Vol. III: 1918–1950, The Lure of Fantasy* (London: Chatto & Windus, 1991), 93.

53 Benedict Nightingale, "Harold Pinter/Politics," in *Around the Absurd: Essays on Modern and Postmodern Drama*, eds. Enoch Brater and Ruby Cohn (Ann Arbor: The University of Michigan Press, 1990), 135.

54 Ibid., 133.

55 Harold Pinter, "Nobel Lecture: Art, Truth and Politics," *Nobelprize.org*, accessed September 5, 2012, http://www.nobelprize.org/nobel_prizes/literature/laureates/2005/pinter-lecture-e.html.

with built-in solutions; [...] The attitude behind this sort of thing might be summed up in one phrase: "I'm telling you!" [...] If I were to state any moral precept it might be: Beware of the writer who puts forward his concern for you to embrace [...].[56]

More than thirty years later, Pinter's initial reluctance to be counted among the political playwrights of his generation, such as John Arden, Edward Bond or Arnold Wesker, had turned into a firm avowal of the sheer necessity of politically committed theatre:

> Political theatre now is even more important than it ever was, if by political theatre you mean plays which deal with the real world, not with a manufactured or fantasy world. We are in a terrible dip at the moment, a kind of abyss, because the assumption is that politics are all over. That's what the propaganda says. But I don't believe the propaganda. I believe that politics, our political consciousness and our political intelligence are not all over, because if they are, we are really doomed.[57]

Unquestionably, there is more than a fair share of blatant sermonising and unashamedly tendentious polemics in Pinter's highly emotional Nobel speech, which, suffused with sarcasm and black humour, eventually turns into a remarkably impassioned indictment of the United States' claim to world leadership and its record of human rights violations. Liberally recycling extensive passages from his 1996 *Guardian* article "It Never Happened," Pinter vehemently denounces American involvement in Central and South America and the country's support of totalitarian regimes from Chile and El Salvador to Indonesia, Greece and Turkey, while successfully covering up its inglorious part in world politics:

> It never happened. Nothing ever happened. Even while it was happening it wasn't happening. It didn't matter. It was of no interest. The crimes of the United States have been systematic, constant, vicious, remorseless, but very few people have actually talked about them. You have to hand it to America. It has exercised a quite clinical manipulation of power worldwide while masquerading as a force for universal good. It's a brilliant, even witty, highly successful act of hypnosis. I put to you that the United

---

56   Harold Pinter, "Writing for the Theatre," in *Plays: One* (London: Methuen, 1983), 12–14.
57   Harold Pinter, "Writing, Politics and *Ashes to Ashes*," in Harold Pinter, *Various Voices: Prose, Poetry, Politics 1948–1998* (London: Faber and Faber, 1998), 74.

> States is without doubt the greatest show on the road. Brutal, indifferent, scornful and ruthless it may be but it is also very clever. As a salesman it is out on its own and its most saleable commodity is self love. It's a winner. Listen to all American presidents on television say the words, "the American people" [...]. It's a scintillating stratagem. Language actually is employed to keep thought at bay. The words "the American people" provide a truly voluptuous cushion of reassurance. You don't need to think. Just lie back on the cushion. The cushion may be suffocating your intelligence and your critical faculties but it's very comfortable.[58]

Only stopping short of comparing the US under George W. Bush to Nazi Germany and reviling Bush's political ally Tony Blair as a "deluded idiot," as he had done before at a public reading in 2003,[59] Pinter denounces the invasion of Iraq as a "bandit act, an act of blatant state terrorism," an "arbitrary military action inspired by a series of lies upon lies and gross manipulation of the media and therefore of the public."[60] While US media and politicians skilfully employ language for the purpose of establishing and upholding power while keeping the majority of the population in dumbfounded ignorance, the country's leadership, in Pinter's view, determinedly sets out to achieve "full spectrum dominance" and is dutifully assisted in this task by its most fervent European comrade-in-arms, "its own bleating little lamb, [...] the pathetic and supine Great Britain."[61] Pinter's political message, poignantly underscored by lengthy quotations from Pablo Neruda's and his own anti-war poetry, very much relies on the idealist notion of the artist as propagandist who strives to appeal to the moral conscience of his audience and to encourage a sense of shared responsibility "to define the real truth," as he calls it.[62] At the same time, it seems highly ironic that, in his proselytising zeal to expose the antithetical patterns of US political rhetoric that reduce the complex dynamics of international relations to an oversimplified good vs evil logic, Pinter subscribes to the same black-and-white worldview as the politicians he demonises. Only a few months later, he would be one of the 420 signatories (among them also Nadine Gordimer, Wole Soyinka, Alice Walker, Harry Belafonte and Dario Fo) of an

---

58   Pinter, "Nobel Lecture."
59   Angelique Chrisafis and Imogen Tilden, "Pinter Blasts 'Nazi America' and 'Deluded Idiot' Blair," *The Guardian*, June 11, 2003, accessed September 25, 2012, http://www.guardian.co.uk/uk/2003/jun/11/books.arts.
60   Pinter, "Nobel Lecture."
61   Ibid.
62   Ibid.

open letter published in *The Guardian* that appealed to the UN to put pressure on the United States to shut down its illegal detention centres and to put an end to the country's "deliberate violations of human dignity."[63]

Elfriede Jelinek whole-heartedly shares Pinter's left-wing politics and critical stance towards US involvement in the Middle East. Her dramatic texts *Bambiland* and *Babel*, premièred at Vienna's Burgtheater and Akademietheater in 2003 and 2005 respectively, focus on the Iraq War and its world-wide media reception and aftermath, most strikingly illustrated by the Abu Ghraib torture scandal and the reported human rights abuses at the Guantanamo Bay detention camp. In a 2004 interview, she expresses her fear of George W. Bush's re-election, confessing that she "take[s] him for an extremely dangerous man, at any rate someone who is a puppet in the hands of his grim aides."[64] Even though the winner of the 2004 Literature Nobel Prize, who like Pinter claims a Jewish family background, abstains from blunt political polemics in her Nobel lecture, there is an unmistakably ideological dimension to her mission statement on literary aesthetics and her remarks on the complex relationship between author, language and reality, which aptly tie up language criticism with cultural criticism.[65] In "Sidelined," she addresses her position as a writer who must stand apart from the "fullness of human life" for the sake of observing the reality experienced by others:

> How can the writer know reality, if it is that which gets into him and sweeps him away, forever onto the sidelines. From there, on the one hand, he can see better, on the other, he himself cannot remain on the way of reality. There is no place for him there. His place is always outside. Only what he says from the outside can be taken up inside, and that because he speaks ambiguities.[66]

Jelinek alludes to the danger, faced by the writer, of retreating even further into the sidelines of today's media-saturated consumer society and thus, from her sheltered enclave, of losing sight of both the subject matter and justification of her writing:

---

63 "US Should End All Illegal Detention," *The Guardian*, March 15, 2006, 33.
64 Elisabeth Hirschmann-Altzinger, "Ich bin keine starke Frau, ich bin längst zerquetscht worden" [Interview with Elfriede Jelinek], *Die Bühne* 11 (2004): 15.
65 Maria-Regina Knecht, "Elfriede Jelinek *In Absentia* oder die Sprache zur Sprache bringen," *Seminar: A Journal of Germanic Studies* 43, no. 3 (2007): 355.
66 Elfriede Jelinek, "Nobel Lecture: Sidelined," trans. Martin Chalmers, *Nobelprize.org*, accessed September 5, 2012, http://www.nobelprize.org/nobel_prizes/literature/laureates/2004/jelinek-lecture-e.html.

Please, I don't want to lose sight now of the way, which I'm not on. I would so like to describe it honestly and above all truly and accurately. If I'm actually looking at it, it should also do something for me. But this way spares me nothing. It leaves me nothing. What else is there left for me?[67]

Even language, which she turns to for guidance and protection during her uncertain passage along the margins of mainstream existence, only "feign[s] obedience. In reality it not only disobeys me, but everyone else, too. It is for no-one but itself":

it runs to make certain, not only to protect me, my language right beside me, and checks, whether I am doing it properly, describing reality properly wrongly, because it always has to be described wrongly, there's no other way, but so wrongly, that anyone who reads or hears it, notices the falseness immediately. Those lies! And this dog, language, which is supposed to protect me, that's why I have him, after all, is now snapping at my heels.[68]

Jelinek's speech reflects the key role that she generally assigns to language in her writing, which has been likened to "a talking cure with no therapeutic end in sight,"[69] mimicking, echoing, incorporating, and appropriating a variety of political, literary, philosophical and pop-cultural discourses. Repeatedly stressing the centrality of language to the construction of the subject, the author thus stakes out the linguistically defined boundaries of her fictional creations, firmly subscribing to the Wittgensteinian postulate that assumes "the limits of language" to coincide with "the limits of the world" when she says: "My characters live only insofar as they speak."[70] As Horace Engdahl, then Permanent Secretary of the Swedish Academy, characterises Jelinek's aesthetics in his presentation speech:

What first perplexes when reading Elfriede Jelinek is the strange, mixed voice that speaks from her writing. The author is everywhere and nowhere, never quite standing behind her words, nor ever ceding to her literary figures in order to allow the illusion that they should exist outside

---

67 Ibid.
68 Ibid.
69 Konzett, "Preface," 11.
70 Brenda L. Bethman, "'My Characters Live Only Insofar as They Speak': Interview with Elfriede Jelinek," *Women in German Yearbook* 16 (2000): 65.

her language. There is nothing but a stream of saturated sentences, seemingly welded together under high pressure and leaving no room for moments of relaxation.[71]

Similarly, in her Nobel lecture the subjective voice of the author eventually disappears amidst the polyphonic chorus of intertextual quotations and leaves the centre stage to language. Language thus eludes the author's ownership and control and takes on a life of its own: "I'm always only gazing after life, my language turns its back on me, so that it can present its stomach to strangers to caress, shameless, to me it only shows its back, if anything at all."[72] Notably, when Jelinek describes herself as "the prisoner of my language"[73] it appears in tune with Harold Pinter's deep-rooted suspicion of the ideological manipulability of language, which cannot be trusted as a treacherous "quicksand, a trampoline, a frozen pool which might give way under you, the author, at any time."[74]

Jelinek's disruptive method of linguistic and aesthetic deconstruction, clearly reminiscent of the impenetrable monologic text clusters of her postdramatic theatre, may have decidedly overtaxed her Stockholm audience, but it was part of an actively engineered stunt of authorial self-fashioning in which the message was underscored by the choreography of its delivery: just like the author is "sidelined" in favour of language taking the floor, her live presence is replaced by a virtual image that ironically undermines constructs of identity and authorial authenticity and questions seemingly absolute categories of fiction and reality.[75] As integral components of a truly *en-Nobeling* media spectacle that apotheosises the author as a fetishised object in a "star-centred economy,"[76] both Nobel lectures by Jelinek and Pinter with their diverse

71 Horace Engdahl, "The Nobel Prize in Literature 2004: Presentation Speech," *Nobelprize.org*, accessed December 5, 2012, http://www.nobelprize.org/nobel_prizes/literature/laureates/2004/presentation-speech.html.
72 Jelinek, "Nobel Lecture."
73 Ibid.
74 Pinter, "Nobel Lecture."
75 Christine Künzel, "Einleitung," in *Autorinszenierungen: Autorschaft und literarisches Werk im Kontext der Medien*, eds. Christine Künzel and Jörg Schönert (Würzburg: Königshausen & Neumann, 2007), 20; Alexandra Tacke, "'Sie nicht als Sie': Die Nobelpreisträgerin Elfriede Jelinek spricht 'Im Abseits,'" in *Autorinszenierungen: Autorschaft und literarisches Werk im Kontext der Medien*, eds. Christine Künzel and Jörg Schönert (Würzburg: Königshausen & Neumann, 2007), 195.
76 English, *Economy of Prestige*, 56. In this context, see also "Fetishising Intellectual Achievement," Rebecca Brown's discussion of the Nobel Prize and distinctly European manifestations of literary celebrity.

strategies of self-fashioning demonstrate that it is not just language that may develop its own independent existence. In the age of what Andrew Wernick has perceptively identified as the "promotional culture" of literary celebrity, it is the authorial image—partly self-fashioned, partly media-manufactured—which, together with the authorial name, "circulates independently of the phantom individual"[77] and subsequently turns into a contested site of multiple signification and discursive power.

Bibliography

Bethman, Brenda L. "'My Characters Live Only Insofar as They Speak': Interview with Elfriede Jelinek." *Women in German Yearbook* 16 (2000): 61–72.

Billington, Michael. "Passionate Pinter's Devastating Assault on US Foreign Policy." *The Guardian*, 8 December 2005. Accessed September 14, 2012. http://www.guardian.co.uk/uk/2005/dec/08/books.nobelprize.

Bourdieu, Pierre. "The Field of Cultural Production, Or: The Economic World Reversed." *Poetics* 12 (1983): 311–55.

Bragg, Melvyn. "Nobel Art of Harold Pinter." *The Daily Mirror*, October 14, 2005. Accessed September 25, 2012. http://www.mirror.co.uk/3am/celebrity-news/nobel-art-of-harold-pinter-561240.

Braun, Rebecca. "Fetishising Intellectual Achievement: the Nobel Prize and European Literary Celebrity." *Celebrity Studies* 2, no. 3 (2011): 320–34.

Chrisafis, Angelique, and Imogen, Tilden. "Pinter Blasts 'Nazi America' and 'Deluded Idiot' Blair." *The Guardian*, June 11, 2003. Accessed September 25, 2012. http://www.guardian.co.uk/uk/2003/jun/11/books.arts.

Derbyshire, Harry. "Pinter as Celebrity." In *The Cambridge Companion to Harold Pinter*, edited by Peter Raby, 266–82. Cambridge: Cambridge University Press, 2009.

Engdahl, Horace. "The Nobel Prize in Literature 2004: Presentation Speech." *Nobelprize.org*. Accessed December 5, 2012. http://www.nobelprize.org/nobel_prizes/literature/laureates/2004/presentation-speech.html.

English, James F. *The Economy of Prestige: Prizes, Awards and the Circulation of Cultural Value*. Cambridge: Harvard University Press, 2005.

Epelbaum, Edna. "The Stage as Accomplice: Elfriede Jelinek's Politics of the *Burgtheater*." In *Elfriede Jelinek: Writing Woman, Nation, and Identity: A Critical Anthology*, edited by Matthias Piccolruaz Konzett, and Margarete Lamb-Faffelberger, 115–32. Madison: Fairleigh Dickinson University Press, 2007.

---

[77] Wernick, "Authorship," 87.

Espmark, Kjell. "The Nobel Prize in Literature." *Nobelprize.org*. Accessed September 26, 2012. http://www.nobelprize.org/nobel_prizes/literature/articles/espmark/.

Feldman, Burton. *The Nobel Prize: A History of Genius, Controversy and Prestige*. New York: Arcade, 2000.

Hallström Per. "Award Ceremony Speech 10 December 1923." *Nobelprize.org*. Accessed February 27, 2013. http://www.nobelprize.org/nobel_prizes/literature/laureates/1923/press.html.

Hare, David. "'In Pinter You Find Expressed the Great Struggle of the 20th Century.'" *The Guardian* G2, October 14, 2005, 8.

Hirschmann-Altzinger, Elisabeth. "'Ich bin keine starke Frau, ich bin längst zerquetscht worden'" [Interview with Elfriede Jelinek]. *Die Bühne* 11 (2004): 14–15.

Holroyd, Michael. *Bernard Shaw, Vol. III: 1918–1950, The Lure of Fantasy*. London: Chatto & Windus, 1991.

Janke, Pia. "Vorwort." In *Literaturnobelpreis Elfriede Jelinek*, edited by Janke, Pia et al., 7–14. Vienna: Praesens, 2005.

Jelinek, Elfriede. "Wir Herren der Toten." In *O Österreich!*, edited by Heinz Arnold Ludwig, 7–9. Göttingen: Wallstein, 1995.

Jelinek, Elfriede. "Nobel Lecture: Sidelined." Translated by Martin Chalmers. *Nobelprize.org*. Accessed September 5, 2012. http://www.nobelprize.org/nobel_prizes/literature/laureates/2004/jelinek-lecture-e.html.

Knecht, Maria-Regina. "Elfriede Jelinek *In Absentia* oder die Sprache zur Sprache bringen." *Seminar: A Journal of Germanic Studies* 43, no. 3 (2007): 351–65.

Konzett, Matthias. *The Rhetoric of National Dissent in Thomas Bernhard, Peter Handke and Elfriede Jelinek*. Rochester: Camden House, 2000.

Konzett, Matthias Piccolruaz. "Preface: The Many Faces of Elfriede Jelinek." In *Elfriede Jelinek: Writing Woman, Nation, and Identity: A Critical Anthology*, edited by Matthias Piccolruaz Konzett, and Margarete Lamb-Faffelberger, 7–21. Madison: Fairleigh Dickinson University Press, 2007.

Künzel, Christine. "Einleitung." In *Autorinszenierungen: Autorschaft und literarisches Werk im Kontext der Medien*, edited by Christine Künzel, and Jörg Schönert, 9–23. Würzburg: Königshausen & Neumann, 2007.

Lindqvist, Anders. "Interview with Elfriede Jelinek, October 2004." *Nobelprize.org*. Accessed September 5, 2012. http://www.nobelprize.org/nobel_prizes/literature/laureates/2004/jelinek-interview_text.html.

Marshall, P. David. *Celebrity and Power: Fame in Contemporary Culture*. Minneapolis: University of Minnesota Press, 1997.

März, Ursula. "Elfriede und Elfriede." *Zeit Online*, December 16, 2004. Accessed January 2, 2013. http://www.zeit.de/2004/52/KA-LIT_LEBEN52.

Moran, Joe. *Star Authors: Literary Celebrity in America*. London: Pluto Press, 2000.

Neilan, Terence. "Fiery Austrian Writer Wins Nobel Prize for Literature." *The New York Times*, October 7, 2004. Accessed January 2, 2013. http://www.nytimes.com/2004/10/07/books/07CND-NOBE.html?_r=0.

Nightingale, Benedict. "Harold Pinter/Politics." In *Around the Absurd: Essays on Modern and Postmodern Drama*, edited by Enoch Brater, and Ruby Cohn, 129–54. Ann Arbor: The University of Michigan Press, 1990.

Pinter, Harold. "Writing for the Theatre." In *Plays: One*, 9–16. London: Methuen, 1983.

Pinter, Harold. "Writing, Politics and *Ashes to Ashes*." In Harold Pinter, *Various Voices: Prose, Poetry, Politics 1948–1998*, 72–88. London: Faber and Faber, 1998.

Pinter, Harold. "'They Said You've a Call from the Nobel Committee. I Said, Why?'" *The Guardian*, October 14, 2005. Accessed September 14, 2012. http://www.guardian.co.uk/uk/2005/oct/14/books.nobelprize.

Pinter, Harold. "Nobel Lecture: Art, Truth and Politics." *Nobelprize.org*. Accessed September 5, 2012. http://www.nobelprize.org/nobel_prizes/literature/laureates/2005/pinter-lecture-e.html.

Reynolds, Nigel. "Controversial Feminist Writer Wins Nobel Prize." *The Telegraph*, October 8, 2004. Accessed January 2, 2013. http://www.telegraph.co.uk/news/worldnews/europe/germany/1473689/Controversial-feminist-writer-wins-Nobel-Prize.html.

Roloff, Hans-Gert. "'Vorwürfe mache ich ja immer, das ist mein Markenzeichen.' Die Jelinek und ihr Theater." In *Positionen der Jelinek-Forschung: Beiträge zur Polnisch-Deutschen Elfriede Jelinek-Konferenz Olsztyn 2005*, edited by Claus Zittel, and Marian Holona, 141–64. Berne: Peter Lang, 2008.

Rutschky, Katharina. "Einstürzende Dramenkostüme." *Die Welt*, October 15, 2004. Accessed January 2, 2013. http://www.welt.de/print-welt/article346266/Einstuerzende-Damenkostueme.html.

Schwartz, Stephen. "Oops ... They Did It Again: The Nobel Prize for Literature goes to Elfriede Jelinek: Sensationalist, Communist, and Anti-American Hack." *The Weekly Standard*, October 8, 2004. Accessed January 2, 2013. http://www.weeklystandard.com/Content/Public/Articles/000/000/004/746mjtym.asp.

Shaw, Bernard. *Collected Letters 1926–1950*. Edited by Dan H. Laurence. London: Max Reinhardt, 1988.

Sisario, Ben. "A Post-Nobel Roller Coaster." *The New York Times*, October 11, 2004. Accessed January 2, 2013. http://www.nytimes.com/2004/10/11/arts/11arts.html?_r=0.

Stolz, Joëlle. "Austria, I Hate You." *The Guardian*, October 22, 2004. Accessed August 24, 2010. http://www.guardian.co.uk/theguardian/2004/oct/22/guardianweekly.guardianweekly1.

Street, John. "'Showbusiness of a Serious Kind': A Cultural Politics of the Arts Prize." *Media, Culture & Society* 27, No. 6 (2005): 819–40.

Szczepaniak, Monika. *"Kennen Sie dieses SCHÖNE Land*? Elfriede Jelineks Anti-Idyllen." In *Positionen der Jelinek-Forschung: Beiträge zur Polnisch-Deutschen Elfriede Jelinek-Konferenz Olsztyn 2005*, edited by Claus Zittel, and Marian Holona, 219–37. Berne: Peter Lang, 2008.

Tacke, Alexandra. "'Sie nicht als Sie': Die Nobelpreisträgerin Elfriede Jelinek spricht 'Im Abseits.'" In *Autorinszenierungen: Autorschaft und Literarisches Werk im Kontext der Medien*, edited by Christine Künzel, and Jörg Schönert, 191–207. Würzburg: Königshausen & Neumann, 2007.

Todd, Richard. *Consuming Fictions: The Booker Prize and Fiction in Britain Today*. London: Bloomsbury, 1996.

"US Should End All Illegal Detention." *The Guardian*, March 15, 2006.

Wernick, Andrew. "Authorship and the Supplement of Promotion." In *What Is an Author?*, edited by Maurice Biriotti, and Nicola Miller, 85–103. Manchester: Manchester University Press, 1993.

Yeats, William Butler. *The Letters of William Butler Yeats*, edited by Allan Wade. London: Rupert Hart-Davis, 1954.

Yeats, William Butler. "The Bounty of Sweden." In *Autobiographies*, 531–72. London: Macmillan & Co., 1956.

PART 2

(Re)Envisioning Stardom

CHAPTER 4

Oscar Wilde's Long Afterlife: Victorian Celebrity and Its Transformations in Modern Culture

Anna Fomichenko

Abstract

Although Oscar Wilde and his elaborate self-fashioning techniques were a product of the late Victorian era, they have undoubtedly created a basis for the phenomenon we call modern celebrity. I have previously looked at the concept of celebrity as a fictional character, brought into a real social context by combined efforts of the actual person (e.g. Oscar Wilde) and a number of "co-authors": publishers, producers, managers, and, most importantly, the audience. Together they can be considered a complex "author function" (to borrow Michel Foucault's term), which is controlled and kept alive by means of publicity and various self-fashioning strategies. However, this is only possible as long as the public persona remains visible—the absence of a mirror means the death of celebrity, its "expiration." In case of Wilde, the expiry date could have come after his legendary trial and exile, if it had not been for his final attempt to recreate himself in "De Profundis"—a love letter and an incredibly deep philosophical essay which provided a starting point for his long and colourful cultural afterlife. In the following chapter, I am going to explore the modernity of Wilde's self-fashioning, and demonstrate how it has been appropriated by one of the most strikingly Wildean celebrities—David Bowie.

1   Introduction

Oscar Wilde's self-invention has been an increasingly fruitful and fascinating subject for the sphere of celebrity studies since the late 20th century. In recent years Wilde has been looked upon as the precursor of the modernist literary celebrity,[1] an iconic figure for the gay community and an inspiration for the brightest 20th-century rock stars such as David Bowie and Morrissey of The Smiths.

---

[1] See Jonathan Goldman, *Modernism Is the Literature of Celebrity* (Texas: University of Texas Press, 2011).

While preparing my paper for the 2nd Global Conference: Celebrity: Exploring Critical Issues,[2] I was interested primarily in Wilde's marked detachment both from his public persona and his literary works, the reason for which was that the image could be yet another work of fiction, brought to existence within a real social context instead of a literary narrative. Having taken this a starting point, I set out to explore celebrity self-fashioning as a mode of author-character relationship. In this case, the public persona can be seen as a product of a complex "author function" including the actual person, various agents such as theatrical managers, publishers, producers, etc., and—last but not least—the audience. I also outlined the basic conditions for the birth and survival of celebrity and gave Wilde's persistent popularity as an example thereof. However, during the conference itself and the long and fruitful discussions after each session I decided to shift the focus from birth to resurrection. The "expiration of celebrity" (rather than its immortality) seemed to be a burning issue for almost every personality touched upon. Undoubtedly, the question of when and why sounds natural in relation to fame and its eventual decline. Is the expiry date found on the package? How can the "product" be preserved for future audiences to see and reinvent? In this chapter I intend to go back briefly to the concept of celebrity as a character, revise the evolution of Wilde's public image and eventually expand on an instance of "resurrection of Wilde" in modern culture.

2 "What Is an Author," or the Birth of Wilde's Celebrity

The view of celebrity as an "extranarrative" character is largely based on Mikhail Bakhtin's concept of "author-creator"[3] who can engage in aesthetic activity only by looking from the outside, i.e. he cannot possibly become one with his creation—the character. The same, I suppose, is true for Wilde, who managed to distance himself as a person (Bakhtinian "biographical author") not only from his literary creations, but also from his own public persona.

To begin with, Wilde's celebrity persona is a significant phenomenon in the sense that it was never actually the product of his literary work. In his case, the public persona was the precursor of his literary fame, and not vice versa. The first image, the first Wilde to come into the public eye and successfully catch

---

2 The paper's title was "Oscar Wilde's Celebrity: Public Persona as a Character."

3 Mikhail Bakhtin, "Author and Hero in Aesthetic Activity," in *Art and Answerability: Early Philosophical Essays*, eds. Michael Holquist and Vadim Liapunov, trans. and notes by Vadim Liapunov, Supplement trans. Kenneth Brostrom (Texas: University of Texas Press, 1990), 4–22.

it, was, apparently, the "Professor of Aesthetics" of the American lecture tour. When Wilde embarked on his journey in 1881, it was already as a walking picture, an advertisement even. He was supposed to bring to the audiences across the ocean a living Bunthorne, a grotesque "aesthete" from Gilbert and Sullivan's comic opera "Patience," generally believed to be a caricature of Wilde himself.

From the first days of the tour he was busily involved in self-fashioning. He was interviewed and photographed wherever he went, exchanged letters with Richard D'Oyly Carte, the theatrical manager and producer of "Patience," and Colonel Morse, the manager of the lecture tour, on a regular basis. In general, the correspondence had two major subjects: publicity and Wilde's attire for the lectures. He appeared to be extremely conscious of both, giving his managers elaborate instructions, which looked almost like stage directions for a play, and acknowledging, although somewhat ironically, the power of advertising. On 2 May 1882 he wrote to Norman Forbes-Robertson:

> I am now six feet high (my name on the placards), printed it is true in those primary colours against which I pass my life protesting, but still it is fame, and anything is better than virtuous obscurity, even one's own name in alternate colours of Albert blue and magenta and six feet high.[4]

Thus, by that time Wilde had already become an active co-creator of his own portrait; middlemen such as agents and theatrical managers also contributed their brushstrokes to the picture. There was, however, another party at work, without which the whole idea of public persona would make no sense at all. That party was, of course, the audience.

By the time Wilde arrived in New York, strong publicity had already made his image eye-catching and, perhaps, annoying enough for the public and the press, to start looking for interpretations. As a result, an anonymous illustrated "biography" under the title *Ye Soul Agonies in Ye Life of Oscar Wilde* was published soon after the "out-of-the-way young man" stepped off the S.S. "Arizona" on 2 January 1882. This pamphlet was laden with caricatures and passages such as the one given below:

> His reception here has passed into the history of this great country. Our love-sick maidens have not extended to him even the usual Saturday half-holiday, and call him a 'perfect raving angel'. Our wives have tea'd and ice-creamed him, and suffocated him in reeking drawing rooms ... Our

---

4 Merlin Holland and Rupert Hart-Davis, eds. *The Complete Letters of Oscar Wilde* (New York: Henry Holt and Company, 2000), 168.

public has paid its dollar to listen to his lutings. Lilies are at a discount in the market, and Western farmers are raising sunflowers.[5]

Another example of the audience performing its "author-function"[6] is that of a group of students from Harvard turning up at one of Wilde's lectures wearing the "aesthetic costume," i.e. the legendary knee-breeches and jackets.[7]

Although the pamphlet and the young men's behaviour were both meant as a rather poignant parody (a mock-biography and mock-aesthetic costumes), they definitely served their purpose and managed to draw attention to Wilde's persona and start writing his personal legend long before any of his literary works were actually recognised (most of them had not even been written at that time). Hence, Oscar Wilde—the celebrity, Oscar Wilde—the flamboyant aesthete may be considered his first successful creation.

This brings us to the conception, the first and foremost condition for the birth of celebrity, which is visibility. Once a public persona is noticed and the desire to interpret and explain it is created, it instantly passes into the hands of the audience: it is constantly referred to, used in print or even advertising (which happened to Wilde on his American tour as well). This is certainly a vulnerable position, since the persona runs the risk of being interpreted once and for all; in that case, the portrait will be finished and eventually forgotten, unable to spark the interest anymore. The question now is how can a celebrity resist this closure and how did this mode of author-character relationship work in Wilde's particular case throughout his (and his image's) life?

3 Staying Alive: Evolution of Wilde's Public Persona

A study of Wilde's numerous biographies shows that in most cases his career is distinctly divided into periods. Roughly, the scheme would look like this:

1. Wilde at Oxford: the disciple of Ruskin and Pater (1875–1880)
2. Wilde: the Professor of Aesthetics (the American tour, 1881–1883)
3. Wilde: the "man of letters" (his journalistic experience, 1883–1890)
4. Wilde: the dandy, Wilde—the brilliant playwright (1890–1895)
5. Wilde: the fallen idol (the trials, prison and later life, 1895–1900)

---

5 Anon., *Ye Soul Agonies in Ye Life of Oscar Wilde* (New York: NP, 1882), 21.
6 Michel Foucault, 'What Is an Author?' *Screen* 20, No. 1 (1979): 13–33.
7 Frank Harris, *Oscar Wilde, His Life and Confessions* (New York: Printed and Published by the Author, 29 Waverley Place, 1918), 76.

What I have just outlined here is a list of Wilde's faces, all brought together to make up his legend. He changed his masks as an actor would change costumes in a play, moving from act to act, never giving his audience enough time to explain him away.

Shortly after his American tour ended, Wilde dispensed with his long flowing hair, his "aesthetic" costume, and announced: "The Oscar of the first period is dead."[8] This inevitably brings to mind the way David Bowie did away with one of his own characters (see Part 4 of the present chapter). A fairly respectable phase of Wilde's life followed, as he married Constance Lloyd and set out to pursue a career in journalism, contributing regularly to the *Pall Mall Gazette* and *The Dramatic Review*, as well as taking up the editorship of the *Woman's World* in 1887.

Nevertheless, Wilde's public persona was still alive and thriving on constant socialising, talking about and putting into practice his ideas on Dress Reform, and, last but not least, his witty exchanges with James McNeil Whistler. Not only did their rivalry find its way into the papers, but it was also put on stage by Wilde himself (see, for example, his famous review of Whistler's "Ten O'Clock" lecture in the *Pall Mall Gazette*).[9] This way Wilde and Whistler successfully contributed to each other's images, each playing his own part in the other's "author function."

The first half of the 1890s saw Wilde at the very height of his fame, as well as his commercial success. This was also his most prolific theatrical period: since the production of *Lady Windermere's Fan* in 1892 he had enjoyed remarkable renown as a playwright. At this stage, Wilde developed his self-fashioning strategy even further: he adopted his writing as a building material for his public persona and continued using contemporary social and literary context as a stage to perform on.

The Picture of Dorian Gray caused immediate stir in press and society right after it was published in *Lippincott's Monthly Magazine*. The novel was open to a great number of interpretations and, as a result, was subject to the audience's inevitable "co-authorship." It was deemed immoral and "morbid." "Each man sees his own sin in Dorian Gray. What Dorian Gray's sins are no one knows. He who finds them has brought them,"[10] Wilde wrote to the editor of the *Scots Observer*. His celebrity almost reached notoriety; however, at the time Wilde still held too strong a grip on his image to let the audience deconstruct it and

---

8   John Sloan, *Oscar Wilde* (New York: Oxford University Press, 2009), 15.
9   Oscar Wilde, "Mr Whistler's Ten O'Clock," in *Selected Journalism*, ed. Anya Clayworth (New York: Oxford University Press, 2004), 6–8.
10 Holland and Hart-Davies, *The Complete Letters*, 439.

explain it away. The disapproving editors published Wilde's letters to them in their own papers, thus keeping him in the public eye.

As for Wilde's other prose works published after *The Picture of Dorian Gray* ("Intentions," "Lord Arthur Savile's Crime and Other Stories," "A House of Pomegranates"), they did certainly build up on his reputation as a thinker and a man of letters, but no less so on his "Prince Paradox" persona. For instance, Arthur Symons gave a very acute description of Wilde in the 1890s in his review of "Intentions":

> After achieving a reputation by doing nothing, he is in a fair way to beat his own record by real achievements. He is a typical figure, alike in the art of life and the art of literature, and, if he might be supposed for a moment to represent anything but himself, he would be the perfect representative of all that is meant by the modern use of the word Decadence.[11]

As far as his society comedies are concerned, Wilde never underestimated the image-making power of the theatre. To begin with, it was a perfect opportunity to perform, for the actors, the author and the audience alike. Wilde was given a limited artificial space and made the best of it by showing both his play and his own image, very much in the same way as modern celebrities—Wilde's best known "reincarnations"—have now been doing for almost half a century.

Apart from that, several scholars believe that by means of his plays Wilde had shaped not only himself, but also his audience. Regenia Gagnier in her materialist account of Wilde and his place in the emerging Victorian commodity culture remarks that "he supplied the one fetish for the audience that would distract it enough to allow his criticisms: an overvalued and exceedingly powerful image of itself."[12] This view was shared and developed in a later work by Heather Marcovitch, *The Art of the Pose*.[13] There, the plays are seen as a complex, multi-layered parody, a caricature of stereotypes commonly appearing in traditional Victorian society plays. To sum up, Victorian theatre proved to be an ideal setting for Wilde and his audience to produce the famous image of the fashionable wit and playwright. According to Gagnier, the social conditions of the late Victorian era "were ripe for posing,"[14] not unlike the tempestuous late 1960–1970s and our own recent fin de siècle, 1990s. Thus, Wilde's prose writings

---

11 Karl E. Beckson, ed., *Oscar Wilde: The Critical Heritage* (London: Routledge, 1997), 96.
12 Regenia Gagnier, *Idylls of the Marketplace: Oscar Wilde and the Victorian Public* (Stanford, CA: Stanford University Press, 1986), 109.
13 Heather Marcovitch, *The Art of the Pose: Oscar Wilde's Performance Theory* (Bern: Peter Lang, 2010).
14 Gagnier, *Idylls*, 14.

of the "brilliant" period provided the public with a subject for interpretation, whereas the plays created a space to act it out; in other words, Wilde was someone they could endlessly talk about, while the theatre was the place to talk at.

As the fifth—but not yet final—chapter of the Wilde legend is drawing near, it is time to go back to the most crucial topic of this chapter, i.e. the expiration of celebrity. I have already pointed out that the complex "author-function," which brings the public persona to life, exists as long as the image has an audience; the absence of a mirror means the death of celebrity. Albert Camus captured this point precisely in is essay on dandyism:

> ...he is coherent as an actor. But an actor implies a public; the dandy can only play a part by setting himself up in opposition. He can only be sure of his own existence by finding it in the expression of others' faces. Other people are his mirror... Perpetually incomplete, always on the fringe of things, he compels others to create him, while denying their values. He plays at life because he is unable to live it. He plays at it until he dies, except for the moments when he is alone and without a mirror. For the dandy, to be alone is not to exist.[15]

However, losing the mirror is not the only risk for a celebrity; losing control over the image might be even more dangerous. This is a likely outcome of a celebrity scandal. If the audience gets a chance to use tragic or embarrassing circumstances of the actual artist's life in fashioning his image, the thin line between the person and the persona is erased. The "biographical author" can no longer stay a distant observer and retain his aesthetic position in relation to his character; they become one. This is precisely what happened to Wilde after his downfall.

During the trials he still was, in every sense, in possession of himself. His replies to the cross-examiner's questions were witty as ever, and his eloquent and touching speech about "the Love that dare not speak its name" became iconic. In a way, the stage still remained his, until the sentence of the court put a closure—a final "interpretation"—to his carefully constructed persona.

After that, Wilde was denied his part in the "author-function" and fell into the hands of the audience. As Marcovitch notes in her study, this was the moment when the press brought up the old caricatures from the 1880s, "returning...to the old stereotypes of Wilde as a foppish aesthete, only this time as more of a monstrous than a ridiculous figure."[16] Wilde's name disappearing

---

15 Albert Camus, "The Dandies' Rebellion," in *The Rebel: An Essay on Man in Revolt*, trans. Anthony Bower (First Vintage International Edition, 1991), 49.
16 Marcovitch, *The Art of the Pose*, 191.

from the placards and the closing of all his plays looked almost like a metaphor for deconstruction and eventual invisibility. The celebrity was deprived of the mirror and, consequently, of existence. This could have been the final act of the Wilde drama; but, nevertheless, he was still to make another attempt to refashion himself by writing his "epistola" to Lord Alfred Douglas, "De Profundis," which later ensured his literary and public "resurrection."

"De Profundis" is an essay and an autobiography as well as a personal letter. As Gagnier puts it, this is "the only work he wrote without an audience;"[17] however, Wilde did need one desperately, and set out to construct it all anew. In a letter to Robert Ross written on April, 1, 1897, Wilde instructed his friend as to the copying and distributing of the letter to a small circle of readers apart from Bosie. He also explained why the letter needed those readers in the first place:

> ...there are in the letter certain passages which deal with my mental development in prison, and the inevitable evolution of character and intellectual attitude towards life that has taken place; and I want you, and others who still stand by me and have affection for me, to know exactly in what mood and manner I hope to face the world.[18]

He relied on this small circle to restore his visibility; it was to them that he meant to present another character to notice and interpret.

This new Wilde was a remarkable figure, humble and proud, forgiving and reproachful at the same time. As a model for the new character he chose Christ, who in Wilde's opinion was the ultimate artist and public figure, since

> ...such was the charm of his personality that those who touched his garments or his hand forgot their pain; ... and that to his friends who listened to him as he sat at meat the coarse food seemed delicate, and the water had the taste of good wine, and the whole house became full of the odour and sweetness of nard.[19]

In the long run, "De Profundis" brought the new persona to a considerably wider audience. After Wilde's death, Ross took up the "author-function" and put a lot of effort into restoring his friend's reputation. In 1905 he gave the letter

---

17 Gagnier, *Idylls*, 180.
18 Holland and Hart-Davies, *The Complete Letters*, 780–81.
19 Ibid., 743.

its title and published some abstracts, leaving out all references to Douglas and, in fact, turning it into a full-scale essay.

The public response clearly showed how eager the audience was to take the brush in their hands and finish the portrait. Once again it turned out to be a picture of a brilliant actor. According to a review in the *Times Literary Supplement*, "De Profundis" was "further documentary evidence as to one of the most artificial natures produced by the nineteenth century in England."[20] Later, in a piece called "A Lord of Language," Max Beerbohm suggested that even Wilde's sorrow and pain could have been for him an aesthetic experience, a purely artistic invention, and that "…while he suffered he was consoled by the realization of his sufferings and of the magnitude of his tragedy."[21]

It was not until 1913 that the full letter reached its original destination. Another libel action and a new litigation were started by an outraged Bosie, this time involving Ross and Arthur Ransome, one of Wilde's first biographers. "The Wilde trials" seemed to go on and literally turn into a battle of interpretations. Unpleasant as it might have been, this step-by-step revealing of "De Profundis" contributed significantly to keeping Wilde's persona in the public eye and thus alive, though, perhaps, not in the limelight his character used to enjoy.

4 Recreating Wilde: The Wildean Image in the 20th and 21st Century

Up to the present day, Oscar Wilde's image has been many times resurrected, reborn and reinvented in print, on stage and screen; one of the first attempts to stage "the Wilde drama" was made by a Dutch author Adolphe Engers[22] as early as the 1910s. However, in this chapter I am not going deeper into the subject of Wilde as a literary character, mainly because this definitely calls for a different and probably wider study. What I am going to focus on is Wilde's persistent modernity and the way that the Wildean image has been recreated and relived by no less flamboyant modern celebrities such as the above-mentioned Bowie and Morrissey, Stephen Fry, a personality who really stands "in symbolic relations to the art and culture" of our age, or a composer and a songwriter from a younger generation, Rufus Wainwright.

---

20   Beckson, *The Critical Heritage*, 248.
21   Ibid., 251.
22   Adoplhe Engers, *Oscar Wilde: Tragédie in 5 Bedrijven* (Den Haag: F.W. de Ruytervan Steveninck, 1917).

Although deciding on one "reincarnation of Wilde" to discuss in this chapter has not been an easy task, I eventually chose Bowie.[23] To start with, it seemed appropriate in the overall context of the volume. Besides, in spite of the fact that Bowie has not exactly been paying direct homage to Wilde as much as Fry or even Morrissey, his self-fashioning techniques can be described as Wildean in the extreme.

Bowie and Wilde have been previously brought together by Shelton Waldrep in *The Aesthetics of Self-Invention: Oscar Wilde to David Bowie*, an elaborate study of the use of Wildean self-fashioning by the 20th-century celebrities (apart from Bowie, the book also features Truman Capote and Andy Warhol). Apparently, Waldrep was particularly interested in commercialism of his subjects' fame, as well as their contribution to building queer identities. Wilde comes quite naturally as a precursor of the concepts:

> If, as Bowie claims in interviews for his album, his tendency as an artist has always been to take high-art concepts and materials and apply them to a 'lower' form of entertainment, then it is in his refashioning of queer performative styles that his importance lies as a key figure in the transposing of the avant-garde ironies of Schlegel and Wilde from one fin de siècle to another.[24]

Waldrep has thoroughly explored the complex relationship between style and commerce, the artist as creator and product; however, as I said before, my own study is mostly concerned with the ways to keep this product on the market.

To outline the Wildean pattern in Bowie's self-fashioning, it would be best to begin with "the moment of conception," i.e. the birth of celebrity. According to Bowie's biographers, his early recordings were mostly of a derivative nature—an elaborate pastiche of influences, not unlike Wilde's volume of poems, which also had little commercial success and was described in similar terms by the critics.[25] Nevertheless, in both cases it was the imitation and reinvention itself that gave the work a "hook."

Furthermore, Bowie, as well as Wilde, relied to a great extent on visual theatrical effects from the very start of his career. He took a mime, Lindsay Kemp, for his role model and hero, and for a while became totally absorbed in the art

---

23 David Bowie died of cancer on 10th January 2016.
24 Shelton Waldrep, *The Aesthetics of Self-Invention: Oscar Wilde to David Bowie* (Minneapolis: University of Minnesota Press, 2004), 135.
25 James E. Perone, *The Words and Music of David Bowie* (Westport: Praeger Publishers, 2007), 4.

of pantomime. This, I believe, can bring to mind young Wilde's worship of the great actresses of his time, Lily Langtry and Sarah Bernhardt.

In the third part of the present chapter I described the way Wilde's biography is normally divided into five distinct periods according to his five major personae. The writings of each period, it seems, serve a very particular purpose: they provide either the building material or the space for the images to come to life and perform. With Bowie, virtually the same pattern applies; actually, it can be assumed that he almost exhausted the idea by bringing it to the extreme. The evolution of Wilde's image looks more like a one-man show with the actor changing his masks from one act to another within one particular narrative. Bowie went further; he was not just changing costumes—he was changing stories and living them, dressing, behaving and giving interviews as each of his creations: Ziggy Stardust, Thin White Duke or Aladdin Sane. After taking everything he could from a character, he would kill it off (a good example is the dramatic on-stage demise of Ziggy at the show at Hammersmith Odeon on 3 July 1973) and start directing a new play. What the late Victorian theatre once did for Oscar Wilde, the 1970s' rock music scene did for Bowie—it gave him a stage for his productions.

Wilde as an artist has always remained indefinable. He was never simply a poet, novelist or playwright; his career was basically that of a performer who made use of almost every art form, sometimes not as a creator, but as a subject (for painters, writers, not to mention numerous caricaturists and journalists). Similarly, Bowie has never been a singer or even a musician—his work combines and fuses poetry with music and theatre; he realised the opportunities that modern media could offer early in his career and started making music videos, which have played a significant part in his "plays" ever since. This can be best summed up in his own short and sharp words: "I'm the last person to pretend that I'm a radio. I'd rather go out and be a colour television set."[26] Hence, David Bowie's self-fashioning possesses two of the most indicative features of the Wildean image: first, its reliance on visibility; second, its unsteadiness, constant change and reluctance to commit to one particular form of expression.

At this point, I need to refer once again to the complex "author-function" which brings the celebrity persona to life. It is, as I said before, generally three-dimensional, a work of three parties: the "biographical author," the "agents" and the audience. This mode of author-character relationship, if not exactly initiated by Wilde alone, was still a relatively new phenomenon in the late Victorian period. By 1970s, however, celebrity management and using mass-media and fandom as a means of self-invention and promotion have become

---

26   Barry Miles, comp., *Bowie in His Own Words* (London: Omnibus Press, 1987), 30.

a common, even routine practice. Like Wilde, David Bowie managed to enter his contemporary context and profit from it commercially, while observing it from the outside. Consequently, they both can be considered, in every sense, "professional stars," who made the most of the social and cultural conditions of their time without being quite a "natural" part of it.

Generally speaking, comparing the theatricality and "commercialism" of Wilde's and Bowie's self-fashioning has already become part and parcel of today's celebrity culture, and Wilde studies in particular.[27] Nevertheless, I suppose that there is still one crucial aspect left untouched, namely the fact that they can both be seen as great theorists of fame and self-invention. Wilde had never based his work and performance directly on a philosophy; his writings appeared as a summing-up of his "putting his genius into life." His "Intentions," his novel, not to mention "De Profundis," all blend together in a theory of art and the artist's identity, although it had been acted upon before it was actually written down. Therefore, such a theory can be considered a reflection on the performance rather than its source. It is, basically, the Bakhtinian "author-creator" looking at his work from the outside, from a distant aesthetic position.

Wilde was certainly an extensive user of this practice; doing my research for this chapter, I found out that, actually, so is David Bowie. The interviews Bowie gave during the 1970s, especially those from the post-Ziggy Stardust era, appear to be a deeply conscious reflection on art, performance, fame and his own identity as an artist and celebrity. Artistic imitation and impressionist criticism, which came up repeatedly in Wilde's essays,[28] have also found their way into Bowie's view of creative work; he speaks quite frankly about borrowing from various sources, as well as "having no message whatsoever"[29] and leaving his songs open to interpretation. In one of the interviews, he claims:

> I really have nothing to say, no suggestions or advice, nothing. All I do is suggest some ideas that will keep people listening a bit longer. And out of it all, maybe they'll come up with a message and save me the work. My career has kind of been like that. I get away with murder.[30]

---

27   See, for instance, Pierpaolo Martino, "The Wilde Legacy: Performing Wilde's Paradigm in the Twenty-First Century," in *Wilde's Wiles: Studies of the Influences on Oscar Wilde and His Enduring Influences in the Twenty-First Century*, ed. Annette M. Magid (Newcastle upon Tyne: Cambridge Scholars Publishing, 2013), 140–58.

28   Oscar Wilde, "The Critic as Artist," in *De Profundis, The Ballad of Reading Gaol and Other Writings* (Ware: Wordsworth Editions, 2002), 174–243.

29   Miles, *Bowie in His Own Words*, 72.

30   Ibid.

One of the most remarkable features of Bowie's self-reflection is that he, exactly like Wilde, constantly uses the word "artist" to describe himself and avoids anything more definitive. He firmly denies any kind of commitment or 'devotion' to the rock'n'roll culture, so typical in most of his contemporary musicians:

> I'm not at all into glorifying rock'n'roll. I am into my own expression; expression of what goes though my head or expression of whatever inspires me to be a creative person in the first place...it's just an artist's materials. Rock'n'roll is the only material that I know is my vehicle for expression.[31]

The next point is, perhaps, of the utmost importance for this particular chapter. Oscar Wilde is frequently assumed to be the precursor of the modern celebrity; in spite of that, he cannot exactly be described as a theorist of stardom for an obvious reason: he established the phenomenon in his cultural context, but did not have the time to reflect upon it and the language to describe it. Bowie, on the other hand, already had the apparatus and made several statements characteristic of the Wildean mode of self-fashioning. Some of them are worth quoting in full:

> Being famous helps put off the problems of discovering myself. I mean that. That's the main reason I've always been so keen on being accepted, why I've striven so hard to put my brain to artistic use. I want to make a mark. In my early stuff, I made it through on sheer pretension. I consider myself responsible for a whole new school of pretensions.[32]
>
> The only thing to do, if you want to contribute to culture, or politics, or music, or whatever, is to utilize your own persona rather than just music. The best way to do this is to diversify and become a nuisance everywhere.[33]
>
> All the papers wrote volumes about how sick I was, how I was helping to kill off true art. In the meantime, they used up all the space they could have given over to true artists. That really is pretty indicative of how compelling pretension is, that it commanded that amount of bloody writing about what colour my hair was gonna be next week...I was a dangerous statement.[34]

---

31 Ibid., 61.
32 Ibid., 29.
33 Ibid.
34 Ibid., 40.

It was only in "De Profundis" that Wilde attempted to look back and analyse his own persona in the same way, meticulously working through each small fragment of his own portrait.

In the long run, both artists turned out to be "their own Boswells,"[35] although Bowie, here as well as in most aspects of his self-invention, brought the Wildean practice to the extreme. The immediacy of modern media, a dynamic and concise form of expression—an interview instead of an essay or a letter—has enabled him to literally follow his personae in their footsteps.

To summarise, the analysis above shows that certain essential features of the Wildean image have found their way into David Bowie's self-fashioning, making him one of the most famous "resurrectionists" of Wilde and, besides, ensuring his own survival as a celebrity. Moreover, the cultural context he found himself in made him bring the Wildean flamboyance and eccentricity to their limit and reach what has previously been called "fame monstrosity" in cases of Andy Warhol and Lady Gaga.

5   Conclusion

In the last part of my chapter, it is time to raise the final question (as final as it can be in Wilde studies): what is it that has repeatedly brought Oscar Wilde to life in our own fin de siècle? Why has his celebrity never "expired"?

One of the possible answers, I believe, lies in the mode of author-character relationship described here earlier. I am now going to give a short revision of the concept. The complex "author-function" including the actual person, the agents such as theatrical managers, publishers, producers, etc., and the audience comes up with a product of combined image-making efforts, impressions and interpretations, the public persona. It is, in its essence, a fictional character which exists within a social context instead of a narrative and relies for its power not so much on any activity (e.g. writing or composing) as on visibility. As long as the actual author stays in control of the character and keeps the "author-function" balanced, he retains his distant aesthetic position in relation to his celebrity persona. However, should a celebrity scandal happen, the audience can get the upper hand and give a final interpretation both to the character and the actual person, erasing the line between them. With no armour to protect him against closure, the latter becomes one with his persona, which virtually means the death of celebrity. To avoid this, it is essential

---

35   Wilde, "The Critic as Artist," 177.

that the character is constantly recreated and the public kept in permanent desire for explanation and thus compelled to participate in the "author-function."

This pattern dates back to the late Victorian period and yet is ever-present in modern-day celebrity culture in its extreme, almost monstrous form, as demonstrated above by the example of David Bowie. The Wildean celebrities are never stable; they cannot be defined by belonging to one entity or another, although easily appropriated and used by various groups; they never commit to a single art form, being concerned first and foremost with expressing themselves in every possible way; they build theory on the basis of practice; they never *are*, but never stop *becoming*. This way, they avoid the final interpretation and, consequently, postpone their own expiration for as long as they can. The public persona Oscar Wilde created has not yet had its final act, and it is unlikely that it will have one soon, despite the endless attempts to explain it away. After all, the curtain is still up, and we are still performing our part in his" author-function," thus bringing new Wildean characters into the world.

Bibliography

Anon., *Ye Soul Agonies in Ye Life of Oscar Wilde*. New York: NP, 1882.

Bakhtin, Mikhail. "Author and Hero in Aesthetic Activity." In *Art and Answerability: Early Philosophical Essays*, edited by Michael, Holquist, and Vadim Liapunov, 4–22. Translated and notes by Vadim Liapunov. Supplement translated by Kenneth Brostrom. Texas: University of Texas Press, 1990.

Beckson, Karl E., ed. *Oscar Wilde: The Critical Heritage*. London: Routledge, 1997.

Camus, Albert. "The Dandies' Rebellion." In *The Rebel: An Essay on Man in Revolt*, translated by Anthony Bower, 47–55. New York: First Vintage International Edition, 1991.

Engers, Adoplhe. *Oscar Wilde: Tragédie in 5 Bedrijven*. Den Haag: F.W. de Ruytervan Steveninck, 1917.

Fomichenko, Anna. "Oscar Wilde's Celebrity: Public Persona as a Character." Inter-Disciplinary.Net. Accessed July 10, 2013. http://www.inter-disciplinary.net/critical-issues/wp-content/uploads/2013/02/fomichenkocelpaper.pdf.

Fomichenko, Anna. 'Oscar Wilde's Celebrity: Public Persona as a Character'. In *The Performance of Celebrity: Creating, Maintaining and Controlling Fame*, edited by Amber Anna, Colvin, 3–11. Oxford: Inter-Disciplinary Press, 2013.

Foucault, Michel. "What Is an Author?" *Screen* 20, no. 1 (1979): 13–33.

Gagnier, Regenia. *Idylls of the Marketplace: Oscar Wilde and the Victorian Public*. Stanford, CA: Stanford University Press, 1986.

Goldman, Jonathan. *Modernism Is the Literature of Celebrity*. Texas: University of Texas Press, 2011.

Harris, Frank. *Oscar Wilde, His Life and Confessions*. New York: Printed and Published by the Author, 29 Waverley Place, 1918.

Holland, Merlin, and Rupert Hart-Davies, eds. *The Complete Letters of Oscar Wilde*. New York: Henry Holt and Company, 2000.

Marcovitch, Heather. *The Art of the Pose: Oscar Wilde's Performance Theory*. Bern: Peter Lang, 2010.

Martino, Pierpaolo. "The Wilde Legacy: Performing Wilde's Paradigm in the Twenty-First Century." In *Wilde's Wiles: Studies of the Influences on Oscar Wilde and His Enduring Influences in the Twenty-First Century*, edited by Annette M. Magid, 140–58. Newcastle upon Tyne: Cambridge Scholars Publishing, 2013.

Miles, Barry, comp. *Bowie in His Own Words*. London: Omnibus Press, 1987.

Perone, James E. *The Words and Music of David Bowie*. Westport: Praeger Publishers, 2007.

Waldrep, Shelton. *The Aesthetics of Self-Invention: Oscar Wilde to David Bowie*. Minneapolis: University of Minnesota Press, 2004.

Wilde, Oscar. "The Critic as Artist." In *De Profundis, The Ballad of Reading Gaol and Other Writings*, 174–243. Ware: Wordsworth Editions, 2002.

Wilde, Oscar. "Mr Whistler's Ten O'Clock." In *Selected Journalism*, edited by Anya, Clayworth, 6–8. New York: Oxford University Press, 2004.

CHAPTER 5

Touching Fame: Exploring Interactional Dynamics between Local Celebrities and Fans in Sydney's Roller Derby Scene

Jade Alexander

Abstract

The contemporary version of flat track roller derby is commonly regarded as a highly theatrical sport that disrupts traditional sporting and gender norms by providing a space for women to experiment with their gender performance, physicality, and desirability. Existing research on roller derby predominantly focuses on either the sport's history, or on skaters' performance of gender and sexed embodiment. As roller derby becomes increasingly popular, however, there is an opportunity to analyse experiential aspects of celebrity and fandom at the local level. Drawing on data gathered through a mixed methodology, including observation, semi-structured interviews, and roller derby media and promotional material, I propose that skaters in Sydney's roller derby scene achieve "local celebrity" status–although some inevitably achieve more fame than others. In this chapter I explore skaters' negotiation of the "ordinary" and the "extraordinary" as they grapple with growing fame, often resulting in assertions that they are just "regular," "ordinary" and/or "average" people. By examining participants' representations of fan/celebrity contact, this chapter foregrounds the importance of touch, exploring how this aspect in particular both defines fan/celebrity encounters and effectively separates roller derby from other, more mainstream and/or professional sports and sporting events.

1   Introduction

Frequently recognised as "the fastest growing women's sport" world-wide, roller derby bouts draw in crowds anywhere from a few hundred, to tens of thousands of spectators, as, particularly in the United States of America where roller derby is arguably the most popular, bouts are often held in venues capable of seating upward of 15,000 spectators.[1] In Sydney, Australia, roller derby bouts

---

[1]   Hurt Reynolds, "Rat City Breaks Modern Attendance Record," DNN, accessed August 24, 2011, http://www.derbynewsnetwork.com/2010/06/rat_city_breaks_modern_attendance_record.

are held in a wide array of venues, from school gymnasiums to The Hordern Pavilion, and the State Sport Centre in Sydney's Olympic Park that each hold up to 5000 spectators. However, even as the literature on roller derby identifies the sport's combination of spectacle and athleticism as central to its rapid global growth, few works have investigated the resulting emergence of fame and fandom in roller derby. Instead, the current body of work on roller derby focuses almost exclusively on skaters' experiences,[2] predominantly arguing that roller derby is a space for the subversion of normative gender relations. As a result, the emergence of a fan-base and the potential celebrity status of skaters within the localised space of the roller derby scene are often omitted from analyses of roller derby. This is intriguing given that the audience has been, and continues to be, crucial to roller derby's popularity and growth. In fact, as a grassroots level sporting phenomenon, roller derby is perhaps more reliant on its supporters than other, more established mainstream sports.

The contemporary version of roller derby is part of a revival founded in 2001 by "Bad Girl Good Woman Productions," a group of women in Austin, Texas, who formed the Texas Rollergirls.[3] Unlike the original endurance based roller derby of the 1930s,[4] the contemporary version, emphasises athleticism as members work to legitimise roller derby.[5] has also emerged as a highly theatrical sport which incorporates the development of skater personas complete with alternative names and outfits. An iconic element of roller derby culture, skaters' names normally involve a play on words with sexual undertones or references to danger or violence, such as Dita Von Bruiser, Meg 4 Mercy, and Scarlett O'Harmer. As a pass-for-points based sport, roller derby involves ten players grouped into two separate teams skating counter-clockwise around a

---

2 Travis Beaver, "'By the Skaters, for the Skaters': The Diy Ethos of the Roller Derby Revival," *Journal of Sport and Social Issues* 36, no. 1 (2012): 25–49; Suzanne Becker, "Fishnets, Feminism and Femininity: Gender and Sexuality within Women's Roller Derby," in *American Sociological Association Annual Meeting* (Hilton San Francisco, San Francisco, CA, 2009); Jennifer Carlson, "The Female Significant in All-Women's Amateur Roller Derby," *Sociology of Sport Journal* 27 (2010): 428–40; Nancy J. Finley, "Skating Femininity: Gender Maneuvering in Women's Roller Derby," *Journal of Contemporary Ethnography* 39, no. 4 (2010): 359–87.
3 Carolyn E. Storms, "'There's No Sorry in Roller Derby': A Feminist Examination of Identity of Women in the Full Contact Sport of Roller Derby," *The New York Sociologist* 3 (2008): 79–80.
4 Keith Coppage, *Roller Derby to Rollerjam: The Authorized Story of an Unauthorized Sport* (Korea: Squarebooks, 1999), 5.
5 Maddie Breeze, "Seriousness and Women's Roller Derby: Gender, Organization, and Ambivalence," in *Leisure in a Global Era*, eds. Karl Spracklen and Karen Fox (New York: Palgrave Macmillan, 2015).

flat oval track as they compete to accumulate points. To provide a brief explanation, a roller derby bout involves one "jammer" from each team (recognised by the star on their helmets) competing to earn points by passing opposing players after their first lap through the pack. The remaining four players—"blockers"—form the "pack" and use their bodies (including hips, elbows and shoulders) to block the opposing teams' jammer and assist their own wherever possible.[6] At the head of the pack one skater from each team plays the role of the "pivot." Recognised by the stripe on their helmet, the pivot regulates the pack's speed around the track as well as blocking the opposing teams' jammer. A roller derby bout is also broken into two thirty-minute halves, with each individual jam lasting a maximum of two-minutes; however, the lead jammer can call off a jam at any time by striking her hips.[7]

The existing literature on roller derby provides either an account of its history and revivals in America,[8] or an analysis of the skaters' negotiation and possible disruption of gender norms.[9] Anecdotal evidence and non-academic sources suggest that roller derby was popular in Australia in the 1970s and 1980s, however, this is not reflected in academic literature. Fan-based internet chat rooms indicate that roller derby enjoyed bursts of popularity in Australia due to the coverage of American leagues on television. There are also indications that roller derby was played in Australia in direct response to the tour of the American roller derby league *Roller Games* in 1966.[10] While the sport had some Australian presence in this period (1960s–1980s), with television coverage apparently contributing to its popularity, the establishment of roller derby

---

6   Melissa Joulwan, *Rollergirl: Totally True Tales from the Track* (New York: Touchstone, 2007); Zach Dundas, *The Renegade Sportsman: Drunken Runners, Bike Polo Superstars, Roller Derby Rebels, Killer Birds, and Other Uncommon Thrills on the Wild Frontier of Sports* (New York: Riverhead Books, 2010).

7   Dundas, *The Renegade Sportsman*; Natalie M. Peluso, "'Crusin' for a Brusin": Women's Flat Track Roller Derby," in *Embodied Resistance: Challenging the Norms, Breaking the Rules*, eds. Chris Bobel and Samantha Kwan (Nashville: Vanderbilt University Press, 2011).

8   Coppage, *Roller Derby to Rollerjam*; Catherine Mabe, *Roller Derby: The History and All-Girl Revival of the Greatest Sport on Wheels* (Denver: Speck Press, 2007); Storms, "'There's No Sorry in Roller Derby.'"

9   Becker, "Fishnets, Feminism and Femininity"; Carlson, "The Female Significant in All-Women's Amateur Roller Derby"; Jodie H. Cohen, "Sporting-Self or Selling Sex: All-Girl Roller Derby in the 21st Century," *Women in Sport & Physical Activity Journal* 17 (2008): 24–33; Finley, "Skating Femininity: Gender Maneuvering in Women's Roller Derby."

10 Neil Donohoe, "Australian Roller Games 1966–1972," accessed July 14, 2010, http://rollergames.ning.com/forum/topics/australian-roller-games-1966.

leagues in Australia only began in 2007 during this contemporary revival. Since 2007, however, roller derby leagues have increased from four to over ninety nationwide.

Considering such growth, it is also becoming increasingly apparent that roller derby is not immune to the impact of what Holmes and Redmond referred to as the "*culture* of celebrity," as people within the roller derby scene—skaters most commonly—are gaining increasing fame and are ever more frequently becoming objects of fandom.[11] Celebrity studies potentially offers the conceptual apparatus to make sense of the experiential aspects of skater/spectator relations in roller derby by enabling the exploration of fame, power relations, identity production, fandom and interactional dynamics found in this growing women's sport.

Boorstin famously defined celebrity as "a person well-known for their well-knownness."[12] Celebrities occupy a public, often esteemed position in our contemporary collective social consciousness; they are "allowed to move on the public stage while the rest of us watch."[13] While numerous definitions abound, "a good-enough rule of thumb would be that celebrity is a person whose image or life has any commercial value."[14] The extensive field of celebrity scholarship provides numerous reviews of the economic, social, and cultural function of celebrity in contemporary society.[15] Mass-mediated, global celebrity is the main focus of celebrity studies and scholars predominantly define celebrities as commodities and products of media and promotional industries.[16] Such analytic works situate celebrity within a complex network of social, cultural, and economic relations and structures of power that are also often founded on a dichotomous framework of fan/celebrity as consumer/producer respectively.[17]

---

11   Su Holmes and Sean Redmond, "A Journal in Celebrity Studies," *Celebrity Studies* 1, no. 1 (2010): 6.

12   Daniel J. Boorstin, *The Image, or What Happened to the American Dream* (Harmondsworth: Penguin, 1962), 58.

13   David P. Marshall, *Celebrity and Power: Fame in Contemporary Culture* (University of Minnesota Press, 1997), ix.

14   Robert Van Krieken, *Celebrity Society* (London: Routledge, 2012), 10.

15   See Marshall, *Celebrity and Power*; Chris Rojek, *Celebrity* (London: Reaktion, 2001); Graeme Turner, *Understanding Celebrity* (London: Sage Publications, 2007).

16   See Su Holmes and Sean Redmond, "Fame Now: Introduction," in *Framing Celebrity: New Directions in Celebrity Culture*, eds. Su Holmes and Sean Redmond (London: Routledge, 2006), 19–26; Marshall, *Celebrity and Power*; Rojek, *Celebrity*; Turner, *Understanding Celebrity*.

17   Matt Hills, "Not Just Another Powerless Elite?: When Media Fans Become Subcultural Celebrities," in *Framing Celebrity: New Directions in Celebrity Culture*, eds. Su Holmes and Sean Redmond (London: Routledge, 2006).

In contributing to this volume, which unites works from various disciplines, and which utilise a range of methods and analytical tools, there is an opportunity to explore a distinctly different dimension to the study of celebrity and of roller derby. Being an empirical study, and focusing on local formations of celebrity, this chapter is both strengthened through its relationship and contrast to the other chapters in this volume. It is also important to recognise that the study of celebrity and fandom have long remained two separate and distinct fields of enquiry as rarely are perspectives from these fields united and an analysis offered that both explore fame, and the forms of fandom which support it.

While celebrity studies, as an academic discipline is advancing methodologically and conceptually, there are limitations to the current body of work. In order to develop our understanding of individuals' lived experiences of celebrity and fandom there has been a call to expand the discipline towards studies that focus on the interactional dynamics of celebrity rather than solely exploring issues of representation and textual analyses.[18] Furthermore, within the field of celebrity studies there remains a restriction on the definition of celebrity as primarily mass-mediated, global, and founded on a dichotomous framework of fan/celebrity as consumer/producer respectively.[19] As others have suggested in this volume—in particular Samita Nandy in her exploration of celebrity, national identity and role of online media,[20] and Mira Moshe's chapter on the Israel celebrity awards[21]—attention to the specific meaning(s) of celebrity, as I explore in relation to roller derby, is therefore essential, as according to Turner, "what constitutes celebrity in one cultural domain may be quite different in another."[22] In recent years, some scholars have recognised celebrity as increasingly fragmented and permeable, manifesting in an array of social and cultural contexts that vary in size, circulate in a variety of cultural sites, and are associated with specific, often "niche" fan audiences.[23] While this scholarly interest has produced an assortment of concepts to articulate the specificity

---

18   Kerry O. Ferris and Scott R. Harris, *Stargazing: Celebrity, Fame, and Social Interaction* (New York: Routledge, 2011), 6–8.
19   Hills, "Not Just Another Powerless Elite?" 101–18.
20   See Samita Nandy, "Mediating Bieber in Canada: Authenticating Nation in Fame," in this volume.
21   See Mira Moshe, "Celebrity Awards, Fan Communities and the Reconstruction of 'High' and 'Low' Cultures," in this volume.
22   Turner, *Understanding Celebrity*, 17–18.
23   See Bertha Chin and Matt Hills, "Restricted Confessions? Blogging, Subcultural Celebrity and the Management of Producer-Fan Proximity," *Social Semiotics* 18, no. 2 (2008): 253–72; Ferris and Harris, *Stargazing*, 6–8; Hills, "Not Just Another Powerless Elite?" 101–18; Ruth Page, "The Linguistics of Self-Branding and Micro-Celebrity in Twitter: The Role of Hashtags," *Discourse and Communication* 6, no. 2 (2012): 181–201; Greg Young, "From

of small-scale celebrity forms—including, "micro-celebrity,"[24] "localebrity,"[25] "ordinary celebrity,"[26] and "subcultural celebrity"[27]—in this chapter I utilise Ferris' concept of "local celebrity."[28]

Ferris elaborates on the interactional dynamics central to celebrity, namely, recognisability, relational asymmetry, lack of mutuality and in most instances, a lack of physical contact or interaction, arguing that such structures can be and are present in mass media generated and local celebrity.[29] She also indicates however, that due to the localised nature, "fan" and "celebrity" dynamics may be less distinct as there is the potential for greater accessibility. However, given the predominate theoretical nature of Ferris' work on local celebrity to date, exactly *how* these interactional dynamics may be or are altered, and what this means for broader understandings of celebrity has yet to be established. As a result, this chapter is both concerned with providing an—albeit limited—analysis of interactional dynamics in roller derby, and with testing the concept of "local celebrity" using empirical data.

Part of a larger study that explores the nature and development of roller derby culture in Australia, this chapter draws on data gathered through a mixed methodology, involving 26 semi-structured interviews with skaters, referees, NSOs (non-skating officials), and spectators, as well as observation and an analysis of cultural artefacts associated with roller derby. Within this larger study, themes such as community, embodiment, gender, fandom and celebrity, and the ambiguous place of injury are explored. In this chapter, however, I provide an analysis of participants' discursive constructions of celebrity in roller derby, as well as how it is presented as a lived negotiation between "ordinary" and "extraordinary" at the local level. In doing so, I focus on some

---

Broadcasting to Narrowcasting to 'Mycasting': A Newfound Celebrity in Queer Internet Communities," *Continuum: Journal of Media and Cultural Studies* 18, no. 1 (2004): 43–62.

24   Page, "The Linguistics of Self-Branding and Micro-Celebrity in Twitter." 181–201.

25   Rebecca Williams, "Localebrities, Adopted Residents, and Local Characters: Audience and Celebrity in a Small Nation," *Celebrity Studies* 7, no. 2 (2016): 154–68.

26   See Su Holmes, "It's a Jungle out There!: Playing the Game of Fame in Celebrity Reality TV," in *Framing Celebrity: New Directions in Celebrity Culture*, eds. Su Holmes and Sean Redmond (London: Routledge, 2006), 45–66; Milly Williamson, "Female Celebrities and the Media: The Gendered Denigration of the 'Ordinary' Celebrity," *Celebrity Studies* 1, no. 1 (2010): 118–20.

27   See Chin and Hills, "Restricted Confessions? Blogging, Subcultural Celebrity and the Management of Producer-Fan Proximity," 253–72; Hills, "Not Just Another Powerless Elite?" 101–18.

28   Kerry O. Ferris, "The Next Big Thing: Local Celebrity," *Society* 47, no. 5 (2010): 392–95.

29   Ibid.

central elements of roller derby celebrity identified by participants, including: the significance of accessibility, and the "real-ness" and "ordinary-ness" of skaters. Through this analysis I argue that roller derby skaters can be considered "local celebrities," while the grassroots level nature of the sport provides the opportunity to examine how individuals negotiate fame, fandom and being (extra)ordinary.

I further propose that unlike professional, global and/or mass-mediated sports, roller derby contributors and consumers—whether they identify as skaters, spectators and/or non-skating officials—form localised "fan"/"celebrity" relationships which are distinctly different from global forms of celebrity and fandom. In so doing, I suggest that the localised nature and specific boundaries of the roller derby scene can enable greater accessibility, involvement, and interactional dynamics between "fans" and "celebrities." Taking an interactionist approach, this analysis will move on to foreground the dynamics between skaters and spectators by exploring the importance of aspects such as "touch" to fan and celebrity encounters in roller derby. It will examine how individuals navigate space, contact and involvement as part of their fan practices, exposing how fans negotiate interactional dynamics and fandom discourses. The potential for contact in the roller derby scene can therefore enable greater analysis of interactional dynamics and power relations present in fan and celebrity encounters.

2 "People Know Who I Am and I've Never Even Met Them": Conceptualising Roller Derby Celebrity

With the growing popularity of roller derby, skaters are acquiring fame and status within the scene, although some skaters may acquire more fame than others. When I asked Pepa la Pow, a skater from Western Sydney Rollers (WSR), what she thinks is the defining characteristic of roller derby skaters, her response was centrally concerned with their accessibility. As she states:

> To go up and to see these skaters afterwards, you kind of go like, "Oh my god! There they are! They-They're like, right there!." It's like that really weird sensation that all of a sudden these rock stars have stepped into your space. And you kind of feel that you're in rarefied air. And you go, "Wow…" So, you go up and you kind of go, "Oh, can I get an autograph?" And I've seen them do it and go, "Wow, you want my autograph?! Really?"…Because it's still roller derby, they're not getting paid for this, it's amateur sport. And they'll kind of go, "Yeah, yeah, absolutely! Did you

want more? I'll get more for you!." And [then] they grab the rest of their team.

    PEPA LA POW, WSR Skater

Pepa la Pow's account is particularly interesting because she situates roller derby skaters within sport and celebrity discourses. Her initial comments and tone imbues skaters with a high level of status, suggesting two categories or collectives: skaters as "celebrities" and spectators as "fans." Such distinctions denote a division between the "ordinary" and the "extraordinary" as skaters and spectators form an unequal or "lopsided" relationship.[30] However, through the interactional dynamics between skater and spectator, Pepa la Pow proceeds to blur this dichotomy as her representation of "fan" and "celebrity" positions are co-dependent and constructed through exchanges and cues. Essentially, the spectators' request for an autograph simultaneous assumes celebrity status, while also constituting it. Meanwhile, the indication of shock from the skater, as well as Pepa la Pow's comment "because it's still roller derby, they're not getting paid for this, it's amateur sport," strengthens the representation of skaters as "ordinary," and most importantly, unlike professional sport stars. Interestingly, presenting skater celebrity from the perspective of a "fan" invites an analysis of fandom beyond the limitations of a single, fixed position. By that, as a skater herself, who is also grappling with newfound fame, this excerpt indicates that "celebrities" can, and often are, "fans" of someone/something else themselves.

This account is also useful in that the interactional dynamics present, while reminiscent of "fan"/"celebrity" encounters also indicate that celebrity is not a static state of being but rather a construction process. Therefore, it may prove more analytically beneficial to consider that skaters (and "fans") are engaged in "doing" celebrity, rather than simply "being" celebrities. West and Zimmerman in their study of gender and socialisation, posited that normative gender performance is accomplished through the routine interactions in everyday life.[31] We learn through interaction with others what actions, behaviours, expressions, and pursuits are acceptable. I contend that a similar approach can be used to consider celebrity. Considering Pepa la Pow's account, celebrity in this instance is, in a sense, "accomplished" through the interaction between spectator and skater as the skater's response to the exchange is in-line with fan/celebrity discourses.

The "ordinary" quality of skaters presented along-side a sense of elevated status in the roller derby scene was a dominate theme in participants'

---

30   Ibid.
31   Candace West and Don Zimmerman, "Doing Gender," *Gender and Society* 1 (1987): 124–51.

representations of skater fame and celebrity. For De-Nominator, a skater from South Side Derby Dolls (S2D2) and co-host of the Viva la Derby podcast, developing fame can be difficult to comprehend, as she explains:

> [Viva la Derby] get like five hundred downloads an episode and I'm like, I like to call myself a D-grade derby celebrity. That's what I like to call myself because I'm not famous in any sense of the word, but people know who I am and I've never even met them and it's because of Viva La Derby...Go look at my Facebook page, I am friends with the frickin' world, I have so many people on my friends list, I have literally ten friends...the rest of them are just people that are fans of the show, it's crazy. It's crazy!.
> DE-NOMINATOR, S2D2 Skater

Gareth Palmer examines the "D-List" phenomenon, a collective term that is loosely used to describe "second or even third-best" celebrities.[32] He suggests that while the composition of the D-List is not precise, it is "sometimes composed of people who have emerged from the audience [and] it may be the closest representation of the ordinary as celebrity."[33] In a similar vein, Mira Moshe's study of the Israel Celebs Awards explores the significance of individuals who are famous for often shameful behaviour.[34] There are potential connections between both these works as the focuses of their respective studies often utilise the media frenzy of poor, shocking, and/or shameful behaviour to capitalise on and construct a celebrity identity. De-Nominator, however, draws on the mainstream understanding of the D-List celebrity to formulate a discursive representation of her movement between the "ordinary" and the "extraordinary."

Ordinariness, according to Savage et al., is a "key arena around which people seek to establish the commonality of their shared position with various others."[35] Claiming ordinariness enables participants to "opt into" a range of shared practices and activities in a situation where the multiplicity of fields may pull them into separate practices. This is because interaction with celebrities involves a "unique tension between stranger (for whom approach is

---

32 Gareth Palmer, "The Undead: Life on the D-List," *Westminster Papers in Communication and Culture* 2, no. 2 (2005): 38.
33 Ibid., 39.
34 Moshe, "Celebrity Awards, Fan Communities and the Reconstruction of 'High' and 'Low' Cultures," in this volume.
35 Mike Savage, Gaynor Bagnell, and Brian Longhurst, *Globalization and Belonging*, Theory, Culture & Society (London: SAGE Publications, 2004), 11.

prohibited) and intimate (for whom approach is required)."[36] To be famous is thus to become a public figure and fans may expect that these public figures should be approachable in ways not normally condoned in social interactions and that may be confronting due to their contrast with local celebrities' self-perception as "ordinary."

De-Nominator, however, opposes her fame and developing celebrity status in roller derby by adamantly stating that she is "not famous in any sense of the word," while having fans is "crazy," and thus a difficult aspect of her place in roller derby to come to terms with. Other skaters described their status in the scene in similar ways. Madame Dirty Boots' claimed that the adoration directed at skaters is "really bizarre," while Theda Bastard frequently described fan attention as "strange," "crazy" and "weird."

As "ordinary" people, roller derby skaters (and other famous scene members) experience a shift in status where the social situation represents the intersection of intimacy and strangeness. What emerges is a strong sense of fame as potentially shocking and something that is difficult for skaters such as De-Nominator to comprehend because of her "ordinary-ness." This, therefore, suggests that the "weird" and "crazy" feeling associated with fan attentions is evidence of local celebrities attempting to manage and negotiate a shift in their social and cultural status, as well as their position and role in interactions.

While De-Nominator utilises D-grade celebrity to make sense of her developing fame and status in the roller derby scene, utilising Palmer's approach to celebrity as a conceptual tool is inadequate from an analytical perspective to represent the complexity of celebrity in roller derby. Instead, Ferris' concept of "local celebrity" is potentially more apt. Building on Hills' "subcultural celebrity,"[37] Ferris defines "local celebrity" as "a more narrow-cast version, in which people are 'treated as famous only by and for their fan audiences.'"[38] Elaborating on the interactional dynamics central to celebrity, namely, recognisability, relational asymmetry, lack of mutuality and, in most instances, a lack of physical contact or interaction, Ferris argues that such structures can be and are present in mass media generated and local forms of celebrity. Ferris also suggests, however, that the interactional dynamics between "fans" and "celebrities" in such cases of local celebrity, which could include local newscasters and amateur athletes, may be less distinct as there is a higher degree

---

36   Ferris and Harris, *Stargazing*, 34.
37   Hills, "Not Just Another Powerless Elite?" 101–18.
38   Ferris, "The Next Big Thing: Local Celebrity," 393.

of accessibility.[39] Furthermore, celebrity at the local level may operate in very different forms and utilise distinctly different media to that observed in other cultural domains.

Importantly, in exploring the nature and form of celebrity in roller derby there is a need to recognise the significance of the spatial limits of fame within this specific cultural domain. Unlike global mass-mediated celebrities, such as Lady Gaga and Andy Warhol, Oscar Wilde (as explored by Anna Fomichenko in this volume[40]) and Noel Coward, roller derby celebrities are treated as famous only by their fan audiences. By that, "De-Nominator" has acquired a particular level of fame—she is recognised and sought after by more people than she herself knows—but this fame is located in specific cultural (including virtual) spaces. Her non-derby self is not famous in this sense, or to the same extent as she may not experience fame in the same way outside roller derby events or spaces as she does within them. Furthermore, De-Nominator's remark, "I like to call myself a D-grade derby celebrity", could also suggest the presence of a celebrity hierarchy within the roller derby scene. Meanwhile, of particular interest to celebrity studies is the question of temporality and celebrity, or the extinction of celebrity. Given the nature of roller derby fame as predominantly confined to particular cultural spaces—roller derby bouts, and online through roller derby specific sites—roller derby celebrity may very well have a shorter existence or life span compared to the individuals cited above.

Other participants defined or described skaters through a discourse of "ordinary-ness" and relate-ability. When I asked SuziEphedrine, a skater from Blue Mountains Roller Derby League and roller derby business owner, what she thinks is the most enjoyable aspect of roller derby bouts she foregrounded skaters' "realness," stating:

> It's just that the skaters are much more, I dunno, they seem like more real people than like, say you went to a tennis match, they just, I dunno they seem like sports stars. Do you know what I mean? So, I guess derby people just seem more real and maybe that's what it is… And they come down and they're slapping hands with everyone in the crowd and they get introduced and I think it's just, I think it's much more personal (SuziEphedrine, business owner).

---

39 Ibid., 394.
40 See Anna Fomichenko, "Oscar Wilde's Long Afterlife: Victorian Celebrity and Its Transformations in Modern Culture," in this volume.

While another skater, Dita Von Bruiser states:

> It is the relate-ability of the skaters, like they, they're not on a pedestal, they're, they look like you or me, they look like your average person... It makes you feel that you can do that because you don't have to be this superior athlete with this certain body type or this certain image...I think that's what makes it so accessible and that's what makes you feel like, "Hey! I could do that!" Because I look like these people and they look like me.
>
> DITA VON BRUISER, S2D2 Skater

In this context, "realness" represents a perceived lack of fan/celebrity relational asymmetry as a result of increased accessibility. Through their contrast with (presumed) professional athletes, SuziEphedrine and Dita Von Bruiser suggest that "sports stars" embody a particular set of traits and/or qualities, to which roller derby skaters, as "real people" do not. While sports stars have traditionally been associated with authenticity and upheld as role models,[41] the commodification of sporting celebrities and the increase in media involvement in sporting celebrity representation and consumption has led to a disassociation between sports stars and "realness." There is also a growing body of work which considers the potential degradation of sports star celebrity through media representations due to the seeming increase in poor behaviour—instances of drug use, domestic violence, racism, homophobia, and drunkenness—having affected the image of sports stars as well as their status as role models.[42]

SuziEphedrine's commentary on roller derby and "realness," when considered within broader developments in sport culture, becomes particularly complex. Here, roller derby skaters are contrasted with the "ideal" rather than the unreal as sports stars have acquired more capital—be that social, cultural and economic—and status. In so doing, it is proposed that the distance, whether spatial, economical and/or cultural—and the unequal relations of power typically structuring "fan"/"celebrity" encounters in sport are less distinct in roller derby. Meanwhile, Dita Von Bruiser extends this to the aesthetic qualities of skaters. Skaters are relatable, real, and ordinary because they physically

---

41   Gill Lines, "Villians, Fools or Heroes? Sports Stars as Role Models for Young People," *Leisure Studies* 20, no. 4 (2001): 285–303; Barry Smart, *The Sport Star: Modern Sport and the Cultural Economy of Sporting Celebrity*, ed. Mike Featherstone, Theory, Culture & Society (London: Sage Publications, 2005); Ferris and Harris, *Stargazing*.

42   Lines, "Villians, Fools or Heroes?" 285–303.

resemble the average person. This is particularly significant when we consider the scrutiny of women's bodies in sport, as well as within contemporary Western societies more broadly.[43]

It is also interesting that both SuziEphedrine and Dita Von Bruiser represent skaters as "Other." They separate themselves from the collective of skaters through their frequent use of "they" to signal skaters, such as when Dita Von Bruiser remarks, "I look like these people and they look like me." This distancing works to both establish the collective of skaters as local celebrities within the roller derby scene, while also maintaining their own status as "ordinary." As even while they reiterate the average quality of skaters, their central position within the roller derby scene results in relation asymmetry remaining arguably present, if reduced. The act of getting introduced described by SuziEphedrine emphasises the skaters' place in roller derby as well as indicates the presence of differential power relations between skaters and spectators. Consequently, while there may be increased accessibility, spectator/skater relations nevertheless remain distinctly lopsided due to their respective roles and positions in the cultural domain of roller derby.

While roller derby is a grassroots level sport and increased accessibility emerges as a central feature of the sport's culture, evidence suggests that relations between skaters and spectators still remain distinctly differentiated. Olivia, a spectator who often attends roller derby bouts with her family, including a daughter of eight, recognises the limitations of contact and familiarity that can exist between spectators and skaters, or "fans" and "celebrities." When discussing her daughter's attachment to one skater in particular, Winnie Bruise of Sydney Roller Derby League, Olivia explained:

> Jess got really upset with me once (laughs) because she said could she invite Winnie to her birthday party and I was like "Well, you know, you might feel like you know Winnie well because we see her at the games but really, you know, we don't actually know Winnie the person, we know Winnie the player." And she was really upset, like "No! Winnie is my friend, Winnie is my friend, you don't understand!," ... in her mind Winnie knew

---

[43] Jayne Caudwell, "Sporting Gender: Women's Footballing Bodies as Sites/Sights for the (Re)Articulation of Sex, Gender, and Desire," *Sociology of Sport Journal* 20, no. 4 (2003): 371–86; Barbara Cox and Shona Thompson, "Multiple Bodies: Sportswomen, Soccer and Sexuality," *International Review for the Sociology of Sport* 35, no. 1 (2000): 5–20; M. Ann Hall, *Feminism and Sporting Bodies: Essays on Theory and Practice* (Champaign, IL: Human Kinetics, 1996).

her as well as she thought she knew Winnie. It was really interesting; she couldn't distinguish between the two. And the idea that even that I think that that relationship wasn't necessarily reciprocal hadn't really dawned on her at all.

OLIVIA, Spectator

This excerpt highlights the relational asymmetry of fan and celebrity relations present in roller derby, while also demonstrating fans' strong emotional connections to the object of their fandom. While we must recognise that Jess is eight, the conveyed sense of "knowing" Winnie Bruise is reminiscent of findings from studies of fan/celebrity encounters.[44] According to Ferris and Harris,[45] a fundamental element of the fan/celebrity dynamic is the fact that a fan will generally know more about a celebrity identity than the celebrity will know of the fan. In this instance, however, it is whether or not such knowing is possible that is drawn into question.

As mentioned above, sports star celebrity has long been associated with authenticity and realness, primarily due to the meritocratic nature of sport and the tradition of performing as one's self.[46] In this respect, roller derby differs greatly. Competing under pseudonyms and possibly developing a derby persona, the notion of "realness" in this context becomes particularly problematic. Considering this, is Olivia eluding to an on-skates/off-skates difference, or to a distinction between performing "Winnie Bruise," and her "behind the scenes" identity? This would be similar to actors who perform a fictitious on-screen character that differs from their real, off-screen self.[47] It is also similar to Samita Nandy's analysis of online fame and offline national identity. In her chapter, Nandy suggests that there is a contrast between "ordinary-ness" on the Internet and one's offline, extraordinary talent.[48] Here, however, unlike the real/ideal distinction structuring SuziEphedrine's commentary on roller derby skaters, or Nandy's ordinary/extraordinary in online/offline media, "realness" takes on a distinctly different dimension as it is countered by the "unreal."

---

44 Kerry O. Ferris, "Seeing and Being Seen: The Moral Order of Celebrity Sightings," *Journal of Contemporary Ethnography* 33, no. 3 (2004): 236–64; Kerry O. Ferris, "Through a Glass, Darkly: The Dynamics of Fan-Celebrity Encounters," *Symbolic Interaction* 24, no. 1 (2001): 25–47; Ferris and Harris, *Stargazing*.

45 Ferris and Harris, *Stargazing*, 31.

46 David Giles, *Illusions of Immortality: A Psychology of Fame and Celebrity* (London: Macmillian, 2000); Turner, *Understanding Celebrity*.

47 Ferris and Harris, *Stargazing*, 12.

48 Nandy, "Mediating Bieber in Canada: Authenticating Nation in Fame," in this volume.

Olivia's reaction to her daughter's attachment to Winnie Bruise foregrounds the performative and theatrical elements of roller derby, while also recognising the limitations of fan/celebrity interactions. This account shifts the focus away from the kind of ordinary/extraordinary, real/ideal, and average/above-average distinctions previously discussed, towards recognising the theatricality of roller derby. Remembering the performative construction of skaters' identities also strengthens an account of celebrity in roller derby as localised and existent within a specific cultural domain, where they are only "treated as famous by and for their fan audiences."[49]

3   "She's Touching Me Right Now!": The "Fan" and "Celebrity" Encounter

Through immersion in the roller derby scene and interviews with participants, access to the objects of one's fandom emerged as a central defining feature of both the sports culture and of individuals' experiences. Having access to skaters may be experienced in various forms, including close physical proximity, having a "lack" of barriers, and/or contact via social networking sites such as Facebook. In this section, analysis focuses on the opportunities for audience members to interact with skaters, even to physically touch them.

Figure 5.1 was taken at the event "The Battle on the Bent Track" in Sydney, Australia, and captures roller derby's post-bout high-five. This moment was emphasised in almost all participants' interviews as a central attraction to roller derby, and practice that distinguished roller derby from other sports and sporting events. As Pepa la Pow, a skater from Western Sydney Rollers explains:

> At a mainstream sporting event they go hide in the change sheds and you don't see them; you don't touch them. They go get in their fancy cars and they drive off afterwards. Whereas, afterwards [at a roller derby bout] everybody comes down and there's that tradition that has come up of slapping hands. And everybody gets down, and you will touch every single skater, because you can stand out on the suicide line, put your hand out and they'll come along and every derby skater will come and touch you. And there's that intimacy that comes with that sort of thing.
> PEPA LA POW, WSR Skater

---

49   Ferris, "The Next Big Thing: Local Celebrity," 393.

FIGURE 5.1 *Roller derby "victory lap"*
Note: Image taken at "Battle on the Bent Track" at the Hordern Pavilion, Sydney, New South Wales, Australia on 16/2/13.
IMAGE COURTESY OF KIM LEE (CAPTAIN SHUTTERSPEED) AND USED WITH PERMISSION. SEE HTTP://WWW.ROARINGSTORMPHOTOGRAPHY.COM.

According to Finnegan,[50] touch has a central place in human interactions and has the potential to be pleasurable, aggressive, sexual, comforting, or even coercive (among other things). As such, touch can also be welcomed or unwelcomed, and as a result, is often regulated in society; defining who can touch whom where, when and under what circumstances. Touch also has a long history in religious traditions and iconic art works—from the *Creation of Adam* painted by Michelangelo on the ceiling of the Sistine Chapel, to the role of touching in prayer and religious practices—tactile contact is often used to represent the union of humans and the divine.[51] As de Witte suggests, "the image of divine touch does not only refer back to creation of mankind, but primarily to the individual believer's relationship with God through the Holy

---

50   Ruth Finnegan, "Tactile Communication," in *The Book of Touch*, ed. Constance Classen (Oxford: Berg, 2005), 18–25.
51   Marleen de Witte, "Touch," *Material Religion* 7, no. 1 (2011): 151.

Spirit in the here and now."[52] This is not to suggest that roller derby skaters are akin to religious figures or perceptions of God or a Holy Spirit, but rather that the act of "touching" has a history of representing the emotional, physical and psychological relationship between the individual and the divine, or the "ordinary" and the "extraordinary." Essentially, touch, more so than our other senses, enables us to establish reality,[53] to know something to be real because it is tangible and, as such, can be, and often is, a factor in "fan" and "celebrity" encounters.

Consequently, the post-bout high-five invites an analysis of spectatorship, fandom and celebrity in a way that foregrounds the related themes of involvement, proximity and embodiment. In the image, the higher vantage point and length-ways point of view enables us to see the unbroken line of spectators around the edge of the track. The lighting also provides an interesting contrast as skaters are illuminated on the track as individuals while the waiting spectators appear as a darker, seemingly unified mass around the edge of the track: standing together, side-by-side, the spectators are all facing the on-coming skaters as they wait with their right arms outstretched. This embodied participatory form of fan practice is thus experienced both as individuals, and as part of a collective.

Other participants considered this tradition as a collective form of spectator contact and enjoyment. Knickers, a spectator and new member of Western Sydney Rollers, presented a similar account when she says:

> You get to see [the skaters] up close, even if they're red and sweaty and stuff. It's a friendly thing, so it's nice to do. And I think if spectators are there holding out their hand, they definitely enjoyed it, and they're passing on that enjoyment to the others as well, and their excitement. Because you run to the line, like yeah! Because you're cheering, holding out your hand.
> KNICKERS, Spectator and WSR Skater

Interestingly, while attending roller derby bouts I often observed spectators' movement from the stands to the track side in ways reminiscent of Knickers description. This movement from distance to closeness—as well as the enthusiastically vocal ways in which they do it—signal a want to be involved in the

---

52 Ibid.
53 Constance Classen, "Fingerprints: Writing about Touch," in *The Book of Touch*, ed. Constance Classen (Oxford: Berg, 2005), 1–9; De Witte, "Touch," 148–55; Finnegan, "Tactile Communication." 18–25.

contact, the event, the cultural mores, as well as to gain intimacy and/or seek a personalised experiential encounter with skaters; to "touch" and be "touched." In fact, it is Pepa la Pow's final comment, "And there's that intimacy that comes with that sort of thing," which suggests that there is an emotional, possibly even erotic quality to touching here. Therefore, looking at this image and considering both Pepa la Pow's and Knicker's accounts, we can see that references to touching can be read beyond the physical act, they can also be seen as part of fans' desire for interaction and contact with skaters, as well as with spectators. In so doing, this tradition effectively constructs skaters as objects of adoration and as "local celebrities."

The ability to make contact with and possibly touch skaters can have various effects on spectators' experience of roller derby. Collectively, however, it can make spectators feel (more) involved in the event, and as Pepa la Pow suggests, can produce a feeling of intimacy. For one skater, the possibility of contact between skaters and spectators at roller derby is particularly important because it puts sport star celebrities within reach and as such separates roller derby from other sports.

> People like to know their heroes or sports stars… You know, we don't run off into the tunnel and don't touch, don't touch or whatever, you know, not really make that contact when signing a hat or whatever else … [And] from what I've seen yep, [it's] probably fairly unique. I don't think there's too many other sports where you can get really close to your heroes. I mean you can't if you go to the swimming championships or anything along those lines, you would never get close. Soccer, again you can't get really close to the players. And I think it helps them feel more involved in, like the game. They can more readily support touchable, tangible umm yeah, ideals I guess, of the league and sense the sense of community… They can feel a part of that community as well.
> BATNATAZ, WSR Skater

Contrasting roller derby to other, mainstream and professional sports occurs frequently in interviews, particularly when discussing contact and accessibility. Ferris' conceptualisation of "local celebrity" builds on dominant ideologies of celebrity theory, namely, that it involves recognisability, a lack of mutuality, lack of co-presence, and relational asymmetry.[54] In roller derby, however, physical co-presence emerges as a dominant feature of celebrity that

---

54   Ferris, "The Next Big Thing: Local Celebrity." 392–5.

is used to signal a distinction between roller derby/roller derby celebrity and professional sports/sports star celebrity. Here, as with the previous excerpt from Pepa la Pow, professional sports stars are represented as reclusive and/or inaccessible. This is emphasised by the frequent references to space. "The tunnel" mentioned above represents a restricted and bounded space, signalling the distance between the spectator and the sports star celebrity. Similar to the previous comment by Pepa la Pow ("at a mainstream sporting event they go hide in the change sheds"), the tunnel is a symbol of professional sport, achievement and capital. BatNataz therefore draws on sporting discourses to articulate her perception of professional sports stars as occupants of another space—an extraordinary space—that is imbued with social, cultural and economic capital and thus beyond the reach of spectators. In so doing, she situates roller derby within "ordinary" spaces, marking it as physically and socially accessible. There is a sense of freedom and fluid mobility which correspond to the structure of roller derby as a "scene."[55] However, we must recognise that compared to roller derby, crowds at professional sporting events will likely be such that gaining access to them is generally unlikely simply due to sheer numbers. As such, the accessibility of skaters is also dependent on the grassroots level nature of roller derby which enables boundaries typically separating spectator from sports star to blur.

The importance of touch to fan/celebrity interactional dynamics can also be seen in the way participants often discussed their encounters with skaters as akin to having "a brush with celebrity." In such circumstances, and like other fan/celebrity encounters, the procurement of a trophy or souvenir often arises as a significant element of the encounter. In the interview with Meg 4 Mercy, a WSR skater, this practice emerges when she describes her attachment to Winnie Bruise from Sydney Roller Derby League:

> M: Watching the Sydney girls, you know like seeing Winnie, you know, just smash it, it's like, you know what? That's what my friend said, she

---

[55] Garry Crawford, "Consuming Sport, Consuming Beer: Sport Fans, Scene, and Everyday Life," in *Sport, Beer, and Gender: Promotional Culture and Contemporary Social Life*, eds. Lawrence A. Wenner and Steven J. Jackson, *Popular Culture and Everyday Life* (New York: Peter Lang Publishing, 2009), 279–98; David Hesmondhalgh, "Subcultures, Scenes or Tribes? None of the Above," *Journal of Youth Studies* 8, no. 1 (2005): 21–40; Will Straw, "Scenes and Sensibilities," *Journal of the National Association of Post-Graduate Programs in Communication* (2006): 1–16; Will Straw, "Cultural Scenes," *Society and Leisure* 27, no. 2 (2005): 411–22.

goes, "Megs, look at her! She's like you. You know, like, give it a go." I said, "You know what? Fuck yeah! I'm gonna do it!"

J: She's an amazing Jammer.

M: She's my favourite! I go, I always go, you know, she's, if I could… I just wanna go get me a photo taken with her or something! You know? I just, I love her! She's so awesome!.

MEG 4 MERCY, WSR Skater

According to Ferris and Harris,[56] fans often seek a trophy or souvenir from celebrity encounters. This may include gaining an autograph, posing for a photo, or simply being able to tell others about the encounter where the story itself acts as a trophy. They conclude that "fans seek and display souvenirs from their encounters with celebrities in ways that ordinary social actors in ordinary public place encounters do not."[57] In trying to articulate her fan-based attraction to her favourite skater, Winnie Bruise, Meg 4 Mercy draws on traditional fan practices. In this context, therefore, the act of getting a photograph with Winnie Bruise is used as an expression of Meg 4 Mercy's emotional attachment to her idol, and presents Winnie Bruise as a celebrity within the roller derby scene.

Interestingly, having a trophy or souvenir from an encounter with a roller derby celebrity also emerged in De-Nominator's interview when discussing injuries and gender, when she explains:

[Injuries are] a little bit of a badge of honour because look how hard I worked that I pushed myself so hard that I fell and broke my ankle, or that I fell and got the most epic bruise on my butt ever. Or, you know, look at me, I got taken out by my favourite skater ever and this is the most exciting thing that's ever happened to me, but she's touching me right now! But I'm about to, you know, get a bruise like you would not believe.

DE-NOMINATOR, S2D2 Skater

Compounded by gender norms prevalent in sporting culture (and Western cultures more broadly), "women" and the female body are often regarded as weaker than men and male bodies. However, being a "women's" sport, injuries—and bruises in particular—have a central place in roller derby as they are used to testify to the female skaters' physicality, determination and commitment to the sport and their team. As observed by Peluso, bruises (and

---

56   Ferris and Harris, *Stargazing*, 14.
57   Ibid.

breaks) in roller derby convey cultural capital as they indicate "one's knowledge of the game, one's skilled or 'expert' status, and one's overall toughness; they may also be worn as badges of honour that distinguish skaters from women embodying traditional femininity."[58] In this instance the bruise takes on a different dimension, however, as it acts as a trophy of De-Nominator's (physical) encounter with a derby celebrity. While a thorough analysis of the intersections of pleasure, injury and gender in relation to roller derby and celebrity is beyond the scope of this chapter, here the "value" of the bruise derives from the individual inflicting injury as well as the injury, or wound, itself.[59] While a bruise may be a seemingly unconventional souvenir, the specificity of bruises as sources of cultural capital in roller derby is what singles out this encounter. The bruise that will soon develop is thus imbued with value because of De-Nominator's appreciation of the other skater as physically and culturally powerful, as well as famous in the roller derby scene.

If we recognise the centrality of spectators to fan/celebrity dynamics and to the constitution of the roller derby scene more broadly, we also need to consider their agency. Even though the post-bout high-five is primarily discussed as an avenue of social connectivity and a way to convey feelings of joy and appreciation, it can also be used by spectators to communicate disappointment and disapproval. When I attended ERRD in 2012, "The Steely Strumpets" engaged in unsportsmanlike behaviour (heckling, intimidation, name calling and "dirty" moves) when they played "The Amazons."[60]

> The atmosphere in the venue has become tense. I cannot believe it, but The Steely Strumpets have been heckling the competition. While their skaters wait on the bench I can hear them calling The Amazons names and trying to intimidate them. The Steely Strumpets' skaters are even becoming more aggressive as some are resort to illegal moves.
>
> A Steely Strumpet skater just elbowed one of The Amazons in the face!
>
> The supporters are getting angry and are becoming increasingly vocal. Sitting in suicide seating I can hear the spectators around me labelling the unsportsmanlike antics examples of "dirty derby." When I asked Lady

---

58 Peluso, "'Crusin' for a Brusin': Women's Flat Track Roller Derby," 44.
59 Jeff Hearn and Viv Burr, "Introducing the Erotics of Wounding: Sex, Violence and the Body," in *Sex, Violence and the Body: The Erotics of Wounding*, eds. Viv Burr and Jeff Hearn (New York: Palgrave Macmillian, 2008), 1–14.
60 Both teams have been renamed to maintain their anonymity.

Deathstrike what dirty derby means, she told me it refers to forms of behaviour not usually tolerated in roller derby: illegal moves, being overly aggressive, dangerous, and rude to fellow members.

When the bout finally finishes, the crowd is steaming with disgust. As the losing team, The Amazons are the first to make their way around the track to give/receive high-fives. The spectators line the track, arms outstretched. As the skaters pass I can hear comments from those flanking me: "you guys did really well, considering," "you played clean, that's what matters," while the skater next to me simply yells out "Fuck ém!." As The Steely Strumpets start their victory lap, however, the spectators suddenly and en masse, turn their backs and leave. When I asked a fellow spectator what just happened, she replied "I don't high five dirty skaters, that wasn't derby!".

JA FIELDNOTES, 29/9/12

The after-bout high-five uses interaction and physical contact—albeit brief—to convey gratitude, thanks, and congratulations as it brings different groups of individuals in the scene together. The collective action described in the excerpt above demonstrates how the post-bout high-five can also function as a form of social protest. In this context, the lack of touching is symbolic and uses the conventions of this roller derby tradition to make a public and collective statement of disappointment, anger and displeasure. This incident draws attention to potential tensions surrounding roller derby's ethos of equality, community and support, to which the spectator's "that wasn't derby" comment refers. It also draws attention to competitive tensions within an increasingly athletically focused sporting scene that are often obscured by the rhetoric of sisterhood, community, and collective agency. Importantly, however, it illuminates the active role of non-skaters in scene-making practices. In exercising collective agency, these supporters challenged skaters' capacity to determine what roller derby is.

4 Conclusion

Throughout this chapter, approaching roller derby from celebrity and fan studies has provided the conceptual apparatus to comprehend fame and fandom in the contemporary revival of roller derby. The findings of this analysis indicate that roller derby skaters are often regarded and approached in ways reminiscent of celebrity, and as such can be considered "local celebrities." Furthermore, as Ferris suggests, in contrast to global celebrities, local celebrities allow for a degree of accessibility as the asymmetry of fan-celebrity relations is affected by the narrowly focused cultural domain within which they exist. As this chapter demonstrates, the potential for contact in the roller derby scene can enable greater analysis of interactional dynamics and power relations present in fan and celebrity encounters, elements which are typically methodologically problematic in studies of global, mass-mediated celebrity formations. Indeed, the grassroots level nature of roller derby predominantly allows for greater access to these local celebrities—through post-bout contact and Facebook for instance—however, there still arguably remains a lopsided element to fan/celebrity relational dynamics. Even though spectators may be able to approach skaters, touch them briefly, and/or become connected through communication technology such as the internet, evidence suggests that they often do not get to know the "real" person.

Bibliography

Barbee, Jennifer, and Alex Cohen. *Down and Derby: The Insider's Guide to Roller Derby*. New York: Soft Skull Press, 2010.

Beaver, Travis. "'By the Skaters, for the Skaters': The DIY Ethos of the Women's Roller Derby Revival." In *American Sociological Association Annual Meeting*. Hilton Atlanta and Atlanta Marriott Marquis, Atlanta, GA, 2010.

Beaver, Travis. "'By the Skaters, for the Skaters': The DIY Ethos of the Roller Derby Revival." *Journal of Sport and Social Issues* 36, no. 1 (2012): 25–49.

Becker, Suzanne. "Fishnets, Feminism and Femininity: Gender and Sexuality within Women's Roller Derby." In *American Sociological Association Annual Meeting*. Hilton San Francisco, San Francisco, CA, 2009.

Becker, Suzanne. "Fishnets and Femininities: Resistance, Construction, and Reproduction of Femininity within Sport." In *American Sociological Association Annual Meeting*. Hilton Atlanta and Atlanta Marriott Marquis, Atlanta, GA, 2010.

Boorstin, Daniel J. *The Image, or What Happened to the American Dream*. Harmondsworth: Penguin Books, 1963.

Carlson, Jennifer. "The Female Significant in All-Women's Amateur Roller Derby." *Sociology of Sport Journal* 27 (2010): 428–40.

Caudwell, Jayne. "Sporting Gender: Women's Footballing Bodies as Sites/Sights for the (Re)Articulation of Sex, Gender, and Desire." *Sociology of Sport Journal* 20, no. 4 (2003): 371–86.

Classen, Constance. "Fingerprints: Writing about Touch." In *The Book of Touch*, edited by Constance Classen, 1–9. Oxford and New York: Berg, 2005.

Cohen, Jodie H. "Sporting-Self or Selling Sex: All-Girl Roller Derby in the 21st Century." *Women in Sport & Physical Activity Journal* (2008): 24–33.

Coppage, Keith. *Roller Derby to Rollerjam: The Authorized Story of an Unauthorized Sport*. Printed in Korea through Print Vision: Squarebooks, 1999.

Cox, Barbara, and Shona Thompson. "Multiple Bodies: Sportswomen, Soccer and Sexuality." *International Review for the Sociology of Sport* 35, no. 1 (2000): 5–20.

Crawford, Garry. "Consuming Sport, Consuming Beer: Sport Fans, Scene, and Everyday Life," Chapter 14. In *Sport, Beer, and Gender: Promotional Culture and Contemporary Social Life*, edited by Lawrence A. Wenner, and Steven J. Jackson, 279–98. Popular Culture and Everyday Life. New York: Peter Lang Publishing, 2009.

De Witte, Marleen. "Touch." *Material Religion* 7, no. 1 (2011): 148–55.

Donohoe, Neil. "Australian Roller Games 1966–1972." Accessed July 14, 2010. http://rollergames.ning.com/forum/topics/australian-roller-games-1966.

Dundas, Zach. *The Renegade Sportsman: Drunken Runners, Bike Polo Superstars, Roller Derby Rebels, Killer Birds, and Other Uncommon Thrills on the Wild Frontier of Sports*. New York: Riverhead Books, 2010.

Ferris, Kerry O. "Through a Glass, Darkly: The Dynamics of Fan-Celebrity Encounters." *Symbolic Interaction* 24, no. 1 (2001): 25–47.

Ferris, Kerry O. "Seeing and Being Seen: The Moral Order of Celebrity Sightings." *Journal of Contemporary Ethnography* 33, no. 3 (2004): 236–64.

Ferris, Kerry O. "The Next Big Thing: Local Celebrity." *Society* 47, no. 5 (2010): 392–95.

Ferris, Kerry O., and Scott R. Harris. *Stargazing: Celebrity, Fame, and Social Interaction*. Contemporary Sociological Perspectives, edited by Valerie Jenness, Irvine O'Brien, and Jody O'Brien. New York and London: Routledge, 2011.

Finley, Nancy J. "Skating Femininity: Gender Maneuvering in Women's Roller Derby." *Journal of Contemporary Ethnography* 39, no. 4 (2010): 359–87.

Finnegan, Ruth. "Tactile Communication." In *The Book of Touch*, edited by Constance Classen, 18–25. Oxford and New York: Berg, 2005.

Giles, David. *Illusions of Immortality: A Psychology of Fame and Celebrity*. London: Macmillian, 2000.

Hall, M. Ann. *Feminism and Sporting Bodies: Essays on Theory and Practice*. Champaign, IL: Human Kinetics, 1996.

Hearn, Jeff, and Viv Burr. "Introducing the Erotics of Wounding: Sex, Violence and the Body," Chapter 1. In *Sex, Violence and the Body: The Erotics of Wounding*, edited by Viv Burr, and Jeff Hearn, 1–14. New York: Palgrave Macmillian, 2008.

Hesmondhalgh, David. "Subcultures, Scenes or Tribes? None of the Above." *Journal of Youth Studies* 8, no. 1 (2005): 21–40.

Hills, Matt. "Not Just Another Powerless Elite?: When Media Fans Become Subcultural Celebrities," Chapter 6. In *Framing Celebrity: New Directions in Celebrity Culture*, edited by Su Holmes, and Sean Redmond, 101–18. London and New York: Routledge, 2006.

Holmes, Su, and Sean Redmond. "A Journal in *Celebrity Studies*." *Celebrity Studies* 1, no. 1 (2010): 1–10.

Holmes, Su, and Sean Redmond. "Introduction: Understanding Celebrity Culture," Chapter 1. In *Framing Celebrity: New Directions in Celebrity Culture*, edited by Su Holmes, and Sean Redmond, 1–16. London and New York: Routledge, 2006.

Howes, David. "Skinscapes: Embodiment, Culture and Environment." In *The Book of Touch*, edited by Constance Classen, 27–39. Oxford and New York: Berg, 2005.

Joulwan, Melissa. *Rollergirl: Totally True Tales from the Track*. New York: Touchstone, 2007.

Kearney, Mary Celeste. "Tough Girls in a Rough Game: Televising the Unruly Female Athletes of Contemporary Roller Derby." *Feminist Media Studies* (2011): 1–19.

Krausch, Meghan. "'Feminism(S) in Practice': The Sport, Business, and Politics of Roller Derby." In *American Sociological Association Annual Meeting*. Hilton San Francisco, San Francisco, CA, 2009.

Lines, Gill. "Villians, Fools or Heroes? Sports Stars as Role Models for Young People." *Leisure Studies* 20, no. 4 (2001): 285–303.

Mabe, Catherine. *Roller Derby: The History and All-Girl Revival of the Greatest Sport on Wheels*. Denver: Speck press, 2007.

Marshall, P. David. *Celebrity and Power: Fame in Contemporary Culture*. University of Minnesota Press, 1997.

Palmer, Gareth. "The Undead: Life on the D-List." *Westminster Papers in Communication and Culture* 2, no. 2 (2005): 37–53.

Pavlidis, Adele. "From Riot Grrrls to Roller Derby? Exploring the Relations between Gender, Music and Sport." *Leisure Studies* 31, no. 2 (2012): 165–76.

Pavlidis, Adele, and Simone Fullager. "Becoming Roller Derby Grrrls: Exploring the Gendered Play of Affect in Mediated Sport Cultures." *International Review for the Sociology of Sport* (2012): 1–16.

Peluso, Natalie M. "'Cruising for a Bruising': Women's Flat Track Roller Derby as Embodied Resistance." In *American Sociological Association Annual Meeting*. Hilton Atlanta and Atlanta Marriott Marquis, Atlanta, GA, 2010.

Peluso, Natalie M. "'Crusin' for a 'Brusin': Women's Flat Track Roller Derby," Chapter 3. In *Embodied Resistance: Challenging the Norms, Breaking the Rules*, edited by Chris Bobel, and Samantha Kwan, 37–47. Nashville: Vanderbilt University Press, 2011.

Peterson, Bob. "Celebrity, Popular Culture and Sport," Chapter 17. In *Youth Sport in Australia*, edited by Steve Georgakis, and Kate Russell, 255–64. Sydney: University of Sydney Press, 2011.

Peterson, Richard A., and Andy Bennett. "Introducing Music Scenes." In *Music Scenes: Local, Translocal, Virtual*, edited by Andy Bennett, and Richard A. Peterson, 1–16. Nashville: Vanderbilt University Press, 2004.

Reynolds, Hurt. "Rat City Breaks Modern Attendance Record." DNN. Accessed August 24, 2011. http://www.derbynewsnetwork.com/2010/06/rat_city_breaks_modern_attendance_record.

Silverman, David. *Doing Qualitative Research: A Practical Handbook (Third Edition)*. London: Sage Publications, 2010.

Smart, Barry. *The Sport Star: Modern Sport and the Cultural Economy of Sporting Celebrity*. Theory, Culture & Society, edited by Mike Featherstone. London, Thousand Oaks and New Delhi: Sage Publications, 2005.

Storms, Carolyn E. "'There's No Sorry in Roller Derby': A Feminist Examination of Identity of Women in the Full Contact Sport of Roller Derby." *The New York Sociologist* 3 (2008): 68–87.

Straw, Will. "Cultural Scenes." *Society and Leisure* 27, no. 2 (2005): 411–22.

Straw, Will. "Scenes and Sensibilities." *Journal of the National Association of Post-Graduate Programs in Communication* (2006): 1–16.

Turner, Graeme. *Understanding Celebrity*. London: Sage Publications, 2007.

Turner, Graeme. "Approaching Celebrity Studies." *Celebrity Studies* 1, no. 1 (2010): 11–20.

Van Krieken, Robert. *Celebrity Society*. London and New York: Routledge, 2012.

West, Candace, and Don Zimmerman. "Doing Gender," *Gender & Society* 1 (1987).

CHAPTER 6

Celebrity Awards, Fan Communities and the Reconstruction of "High" and "Low" Cultures

Mira Moshe

Abstract

Societies tend to honour their prominent citizens for unique contributions to the community by means of awarding various prestigious prizes. The prize-giving ceremony has much symbolic value since it is an attempt to cope with cultural relativism and preserve functionalism and social structuralism. Israeli society honours its prominent sons and daughters by means of awarding the Israel Prize to citizens who excel in their field and make ground-breaking contributions to society. The prize-giving ceremony is held each year at the culmination of the Independence Day festivities in Jerusalem. At the exact same moment, an alternative ceremony takes place every year on the "Gossip and Entertainment" internet site, which honours Israeli celebrities by bestowing the "Israel Celeb Awards" to denizens of the swamp who show outstanding accomplishments in the entertainment world. Whereas in the first instance the prize symbolises respect and gratitude for activities performed in the highest scientific and cultural echelons of the country, the second instance involves a vehicle for making fun of local celebs This chapter will show how what began as an attempt to sarcastically emphasize the gap between "high culture" and "low culture" ended up inspiring a conceptual dialogue between "admirers" and "objectors," replacing a discussion of cultural quality with an internal squabble among fans.

1   Introduction

Fandom is a common feature of popular culture in industrial societies. It selects certain performers, narratives or genres from the repertoire of mass-produced and mass-distributed entertainment and takes them into the culture of a self-selected faction of people.[1] By participating in fandom, fans construct

---

1 John Fiske, "The Cultural Economy of Fandom," in *The Adoring Audience: Fan Culture and Popular Media*, ed. L. Lewis (London: Routledge, 1992), 30–49.

coherent identities for themselves,[2] while restoring, negotiating or subverting their idols' national identity.[3] Thus, fandom—a collective of people who interact together on the basis of a specific media artefact—includes the intense involvement of the fans and the interaction of those fans not just with the artefact itself but with one another.[4] But what is the nature of these interactions? What is the significance inherent in being part of the fan community and how is the fandom discourse constructed in and between fan communities?

2   Celebrities and the Fan Community

Being a "fan" means participating in a range of activities that extend beyond the private realm and reflect an enhanced emotional involvement. Such activities may include purchasing or subscribing to fan magazines, writing letters to actors, producers, writers or fan publications, conversing with other fans, joining fan clubs, attending fan events, and so on.[5] Hence, fans are often viewed as distinct social groups with important in-group identities that are active in the construction of media identities,[6] while also potentially functioning as an alternative social community.[7] Members of fan communities tend to project multiple selves. They separate their private lives as fans from their public and work personae.[8] The more dedicated they are, the more they value their celebrity worship and develop an interest in the circumstances of film or TV productions, relationships among fictional characters and celebrities'

---

2   Lawrence Grossberg, "Is There a Fan in the House?: The Affective Sensibility of Fandom," in *The Adoring Audience: Fan Culture and Popular Media*, ed. L. Lewis (London: Routledge, 1992), 50–68.

3   Samita Nandy, "Fame and Nation: National Identity of Pop Star Justin Bieber," in *The Performance of Celebrity*, ed. Amber A. Colvin (Oxford, UK: Inter-Disciplinary Press, 2013), 13–21.

4   Kari Whittenberger-Keith, "Understanding Fandom Rhetorically: The Case of 'Beauty and the Beast,'" in *Postmodern Political Communication: The Fringe Challenges the Center*, ed. Andrew King (Santa Barbara, CA: Praeger Publishers, 1992), 131–52.

5   Denise D. Bielby, Lee C. Harrington and William T. Bielby, "Whose Stories Are They? Fans' Engagement with Soap Opera Narratives in Three Sites of Fan Activity," *Journal of Broadcasting and Electronic Media* 43 (1999): 35–51.

6   Scott K. Radford and Peter H. Bloch, "Grief, Commiseration, and Consumption Following the Death of a Celebrity," *Journal of Consumer Culture* 12, no. 2 (2012): 137–55.

7   Henry Jenkins, *Textual Poachers: Television Fans and Participatory Culture* (New York: Routledge, 1992).

8   Kent L. Sandstrom, Daniel D. Martin and Gary Alan Fine, *Symbols, Selves, and Social Reality* (New York: Oxford University Press, 2006).

off-screen lives.[9] At the same time, strong empathy and emulation of celebrities' values and beliefs can lead to involvement in a social network or community of shared values exemplified by the celebrity.[10] Those disenfranchised and marginalised economically or socially, those who feel they do not have a voice, those who feel loss or a diminished sense of identity and those who feel powerless to deal with fragmenting social structures such as family, religious groups and community are all especially vulnerable to celebrities' influence. Hence, the essence of fan communities rests in the ability to demark, emphasise and guard the boundaries between the fan community and the rest of the world.[11] These boundaries, which allow the identification both with the object of fandom (e.g., the celebrity) and the community of fans, are central to the experience of fandom.[12] But where do fan communities operate? Where do they get together in order to maintain their social activities, frame their inner discourse and re-establish in-group narratives?

The internet is nowadays one of the most prominent platforms generating fan communities, supporting a dialogue between these communities and generally enabling intercultural fan activity. It allows the construction of a virtual community based upon gender, fields of interests, cultural context and so on.[13] A sense of in-group similarity is formed via discourse within virtual communities.[14] However, fans in virtual communities are less "bound" to one other than they are tied to the object of their obsession.[15] Moreover, the participatory experience between the fan and the media text takes place primarily within a community of other fans or "excessive readers."[16] Therefore, members of online communities are aware of its role as a readership for speculations, observations

---

9   Carine Lee Harrington and Denise D. Bielby, *Soap Fans: Pursuing Pleasure and Making Meaning in Everyday Life* (Philadelphia: Temple University Press, 1995).

10 Fraser Benson and William Brown, "Media, Celebrities and Social Influence: Identification with Elvis Presley," *Mass Communication & Society* 5 (2002): 183–207.

11 John Fiske, "The Cultural Economy of Fandom," in *The Adoring Audience: Fan Culture and Popular Media*, ed. L. Lewis (London: Routledge, 1992), 30–49.

12 Charles Soukup, "Hitching a Ride on a Star: Celebrity, Fandom, and Identification on the World Wide Web," *Southern Communication Journal* 71, no. 4 (2006): 319–37.

13 Fabienne Darling-Wolf, "Virtually Multicultural: Trans-Asian Identity and Gender in an International Fan Community of a Japanese Star," *New Media Society* 6, no. 4 (2004): 507–28.

14 Nancy K. Baym, *Tune In, Log On: Soaps, Fandom, and Online Community* (Thousand Oaks, CA: Sage, 2000).

15 Cindy M. Bird, "Phenomenological Realities or Quinntown: Life in a Cyber Community," *Journal of American and Comparative Cultures* 25 (2002): 32–7.

16 Soukup, "Hitching a Ride on a Star," 319–37.

and commentaries.[17] Fans experience emotions that are not simply inherent, but are negotiated, articulated and constructed with heightened self-reflection in the interactive spaces of the online community. On this plane of interaction with fellow fans, members' emotional and personal life finds its most routine expression,[18] as these fan communities tend to conventionalise group-specific representations.[19] In this manner the World Wide Web offers new ways of disseminating fan-oriented texts, creating identification within fan communities and presumably generating unique associations between fans and celebrities.[20] From the moment when fan communities moved on-line and entered the postmodern age, they discovered much easier access to source texts and reproductive tools. Furthermore, the postmodern nature of the internet acts as a space for the production of counter-publics, thus allowing fan communities to create more complex and numerous constructions.[21] At the same time, while generating unsolved paradoxes, the postmodern condition also allows a certain flexibility and ambiguity[22] by blurring the boundaries between "high" and "low" culture.

3 "Prized" Celebrities

The distinction between "low" and "high" culture is not easily defined.[23] It seems as though there is no longer a stable hierarchy of values ranging from "low" to "high" culture,[24] as the same codes and conventions may be applied to both.[25] Yet "high" art still appeals to a limited but select audience and offers emotional

---

17 Matt Hills, *Fan Cultures* (London: Routledge, 2002).
18 Sudha Rajagopalan, "Shahrukh Khan as Media Text: Celebrity, Identity and Emotive Engagement in a Russian Online Community," *Celebrity Studies* 2, no. 3 (2011): 263–76.
19 Nancy K. Baym, "The Emergence of Community in Computer-Mediated Communication," in *Cybersociety: Computer-Mediated Communication and Community*, ed. S. Jones (Thousand Oaks, CA: Sage, 1995), 138–63.
20 Soukup, "Hitching a Ride on a Star," 319–37.
21 Kristina Busse and Karen Hellekson, eds., *Fan Fiction and Fan Communities in the Age of the Internet: New Essays* (Jefferson, NC: McFarland Company, Inc., Publishers, 2006).
22 Calvin Morrill and William Bailey, "The Reciprocal Power Identities and Social Style: A Note on a Specimen Deviant Youth Group," in *Postmodern Political Communication: The Fringe Challenges the Center*, ed. Andrew King (Westport, CT: Praeger Publishers, 1992), 32–57.
23 Herbert Gans, *Popular Culture and High Culture: An Analysis and Evaluation of Taste* (New York: Basic Books, 1999).
24 John Frow, *Cultural Studies and Cultural Value* (Oxford: Clarendon Press, 1995).
25 Terry Eagleton, *Literacy Theory: An Introduction* (Oxford: Basil Blackwell, 1996).

and intellectual stimulation, whereas "low" culture has a clear affinity with the world of consumerism and the pleasures derived from it.[26] Thus the tension between kitsch and culture gradually causes an unbridgeable gap.[27] The manner in which a culture attempts to differentiate between "high" and "low" is often determined by an attempt to preserve these distinctions by means of prize-giving. The Nobel Prize, for instance, awarded by the Swedish Academy in a highly ritualised and archaic ceremony, is considered the most prestigious, financially rewarding accolade.[28] The value of the social or cultural contributions of prize winners is measured by means of the prize's monetary value: the higher the monetary value, the higher the social value. In the Israeli case, one of the most prestigious prizes is the Israel Prize. In 1953 the Israeli government's then minister of education established a prize to be awarded to Israeli citizens who had displayed particular excellence, made a breakthrough in their field or contributed greatly to Israeli society. The prize-giving ceremony takes place every year as the culmination of the Independence Day celebrations in the capital, Jerusalem, at an official ceremony attended by the president, the prime minister, the speaker of the Knesset, the chief justice, the mayor of Jerusalem and the minister of education. The major areas in which the prize is awarded are Jewish studies, the humanities and the social sciences; life sciences and exact sciences; culture and the arts. In addition, a special prize is awarded for a life-long project that has made a special contribution to the state and to society. From 1953 until the present day, 623 prizes have been awarded. The monetary value has increased over the years and currently stands at 75,000 ILS (13,800 GBP).[29] In Israel, as in other countries, the scientific community holds this prize in high esteem.

The professional and social honour bestowed upon prize winners is not reserved for scientists only. The arts also impart great importance to prizes, even if they constitute a more fluid, less organised area, which by its very nature is sensitive to its surroundings; thus giving recognition to a person's work constitutes a prize in itself.[30] The music industry, for example, awards

---

26 David Gurevitz and Dan Arav, *Encyclopedia of Ideas* (Tel Aviv: Babel and Yedioth Media Group, 2012) [Hebrew]; Umberto Eco, *The Open Work* (Cambridge, MA: Harvard University Press, 1989).
27 Theodor W. Adorno, *Minima Moralia* (London: Verso, 1974).
28 Sandra Mayer, "EnNobeling Literary Celebrity: Authorial Self-Fashioning in the Nobel Lectures of Elfriede Jelinek and Harold Pinter," in *The Performance of Celebrity*, ed. Amber A. Colvin (Oxford: Inter-Disciplinary Press, 2013), 67–80.
29 Mira Moshe and Nicoleta Corbu, eds., *The Walk of Shame* (New York, NY: Nova Science Publishers, 2013).
30 Nathalie Heinich, "The Sociology of Vocational Prizes: Recognition as Esteem," *Theory Culture Society* 26 (2009): 85–107.

prizes of varying monetary value for both *highbrow* and *lowbrow* cultural products.[31] At the same time, it is important to note that in both these cases, winning a prize generally has a positive influence on selling the product for which the prize was awarded. Furthermore, in the case of *lowbrow* products, television exposure inevitably boosts sales of a creation having entertainment value.[32] Thus, through organisational charts and websites, media releases and marketing material, as well as public recognition though awards, prizes and citations, prominent figures are recognised and rewarded for their work, influence and authority.[33]

However, prizes may also be given in order to denigrate candidates rather than glorify them. One example of this is the Israel Celebs Awards. In 2009, Ynet, Israel's largest and most popular news and content website, established a prize for Israeli celebrities who perhaps have not found a cure for cancer or established a school, but in their own way these denizens of the swamp have also made a contribution to Israeli society.[34] In order to honour them, Y-net's gossip and entertainment column began awarding prizes to Israel's outstanding celebs—the Israel Celebs Awards. The award-giving ceremony takes place on Israel's Independence Day by means of publishing a list of winners. This ceremony is the ultimate representation of the *walk of shame*—shaking off the shackles of political correctness and turning shameful behaviour from a source of embarrassment into a success story.[35]

4 Critical Irony Discourse and the Justification for Awarding Prizes

Awarding prizes to those identified as belonging to either "high" or "low" culture demands justification. However, while the justification for awarding the Israel Prize focuses on glorifying the actions of the prize winner and exalting his/her

---

[31] Tom F.M. Ter Bogt, Juul Mulder, Quinten A.W. Raaijmakers and Saoirse Nic Gabhainn, "Moved by Music: A Typology of Music Listeners," *Psychology of Music* 39 (2011): 147–63; Richard A. Peterson, "Understanding Audience Segmentation: From Elite and Mass to Omnivore and Univore," *Poetics* 21 (1992): 24–58.

[32] John Ashworth, Jaime C. Confer, Cari Goetz and David Buss, "Expert Judgments and the Demand for Novels in Flanders," *Journal of Cultural Economics* 34 (2010): 197–218.

[33] Tanya Fitzgerald and Julia Savage, "Beyond Anonymity and the Everyday: Celebrity and the Capture of Educational Leadership," *Educational Review* 66, no. 1 (2014): 46–58.

[34] For further information, see: http://www.ynet.co.il/articles/0,7340,L-3707536,00.html.

[35] Mira Moshe, "The 'Israel Celebs Awards': The Walk of Shame on the Way to Fame," in *The Walk of Shame*, eds. Mira Moshe and Nicoleta Corbu (New York, NY: Nova Science Publishers, 2013), 77–92.

name, the justification for awarding the Israel Celebs Award focuses on humiliating the prize winner through cynical and ironical denigration. This is accomplished by providing claims that seemingly praise the said celebrity.

Between the years 2009–2012, forty men (84% of total winners) and eight women (16% of total winners) were awarded the Israel Prize. During that same period, six men (22% of total winners) and twenty-two women (78% of total winners) won the Israel Celebs Award. Clearly far more men than women have won the Israel Prize, while a vast majority of women have won the Israel Celebs Award. Due to lack of space, this chapter will focus on the justification for awarding the Israel Prize for the years 2009 and 2012 only, and the justification for awarding the Israel Celebs Awards for those same years.

In 2009 there were fourteen Israel Prize winners from the fields of science, humanities and social activism, comprising twelve men and two women. Among the winners was Prof. Reuven Tsur. Prof. Tsur is among Israel's most important researchers in the field of literature, and is well-known both locally and internationally as an extremely original theoretician.[36] Publishing houses and authors generally create and disseminate the image of the literary celebrity.[37] This is an economic process in which the literary celeb is a product marketed to the public, generally members of the middle classes.[38] However, Prof. Tsur, a literary scholar and critic with a local and international reputation, in other words, a respected figure in his own field, does not enjoy celebrity status in the eyes of the general public. As opposed to celebrities who owe their fame to the mass media and whose charismatic image is a household word, the academic elite enjoys charisma whose source is their professional authority as perceived by members of their own community. Furthermore, as opposed to the number of Nobel Prize winners, who invested considerable effort in focusing media interest in their image and personalities,[39] winners of the Israel Prize behave in a far less arrogant manner, as might be expected of intellectual communities that tend not to form close ties among their members[40] and do not act to create groups of supporters that would further their public image.

---

36   For further information, see: http://Cms.Education.Gov.Il/Educationcms/Units/Prasisrael/Prashtashsath/Reuvenzur/Nsreuvenzur.Htm.
37   Joe Moran, *Star Authors: Literary Celebrity in America* (London: Pluto Press, 2000).
38   Lorraine Mary York, *Literary Celebrity in Canada* (Toronto: University of Toronto Press, 2007).
39   Mayer, "En*Nobel*ing Literary Celebrity," 67–80.
40   Zachery R. Williams, *In Search of the Talented Tenth: Howard University Public Intellectuals and the Dilemmas of Race, 1926–1970* (Colombia, MI: University of Missouri Press, 2009).

In that same year, seven celebrities were deemed worthy of receiving the Israel Celebs Award, among them six women and one man. Among the winners were Shifra Korenfeld (who won due to her contribution to the Israeli media market) and Einav Bublil (who won a "lifetime achievement award" due to her special contribution to society and the state). Both winners had competed head to head during the first season of the reality show "Big Brother." At the end of the season's broadcasts, Shifra was the one to win the first prize of 1 million ILS. In the course of the broadcasts, much tension was created between Shifra, who was presented as elitist, arrogant and cold, and Einav, who was presented as common, vulgar and good-hearted. Thus the chief drama that was generated by that season of "Big Brother" (which is considered to belong to a low cultural genre) stemmed from the clash between high and low, between elitist and plebeian. The power of the drama and its characteristics continued to have its effect even after the season ended and the two protagonists moved out of the Big Brother house. Among other things, this was expressed in the judges' justifications for awarding the Israel Celebs Awards. The judges' justification for giving Shifra Korenfeld the award was thus:

> Korenfeld, a Jerusalem "underdog," struggled with all her might against the Bublil family and represented fifty per cent of the population, who supported her hysterically. With internal calm and quiet tones, she succeeded in replacing Ninette (a well-known actress and singer) as the Israeli Cinderella, and even to catch a high-quality man who answers to the name of Muli Segev. For all of these accomplishments, Ms. Korenfeld was chosen as eligible to receive the Israel Prize in the field of communications on the 61st anniversary of the State of Israel.[41]

And the judges' justification for giving Einav Bublil the award was:

> With unusual sensitivity and while remaining cool and collected, Bublil succeeded in uniting the nation in favour of her speedy marriage, despite the Gaza War, which stole the thunder from the event. In addition, she succeeded in applying the principles of public relations, maintaining her media persona and strengthening the nation's Jewish identity by means of Rabbi Pinto (a Kabbalistic rabbi). The judges added to their reasons for their choice that in a world ruled by passing fads, Ms. Bublil became a unique phenomenon in the cultural world. For all these reasons,

---

41   For further information, see: http://www.Ynet.Co.Il/Articles/0,7340,L-3707536,00.Html.

Ms. Bublil was found worthy of receiving a lifetime achievement award on the 61st anniversary of the State of Israel.[42]

In Israeli media discourse, Einav Bublil's image was formulated as a "popular" local character who marketed authenticity by appealing to miracle rabbis. In contemporary popular media and culture, authenticity is often a marker of cultural distinction that acts as a kind of popular capital.[43] So, in the spirit of Bourdieu's ideas, the media representation of the authentic allows the acquisition of cultural as well as financial capital by groups lacking such power. Conversely, as part of the local dialectic, Shifra Korenfeld was presented as a universal, elitist figure attempting to preserve and improve her position even further. It appears that this is a significant modern strategy of structuralist binary conflict in which the genuine, truthful, kind-hearted yet hot-tempered representative challenged Shifra, the distant, cold, elitist and arrogant prototype.

However, since the Israel Celebs Awards makes fun of representatives of all social classes and contributes to blurring the distinctions among them, in some way it seems that in both cases, the high and the low, being in a romantic relationship is crucial for preserving the Israeli woman's right to celebrity status. Since both of them met their spouses shortly after achieving celebrity status, the panel of judges that chose both Shifra Korenfeld and Einav Bublil as worthy of the award chose to involve these celebrities in a Cinderella marriage fantasy. From being anonymous, unmarried single young women, they both become public figures, thus, according to the judges, their life stories turn to a fantasy story. Furthermore, since we dream about specific difficulties that we must cope with in our daily lives, celebrities such as Einav Bublil have succeeded by their embarrassing behaviour in coping with those same human difficulties[44]—weight gain issues, challenges of motherhood, and so on. As women well-schooled in the psychology of publicity seekers, both of them managed to obtain romantic advantages cheered on by their many admirers. On the other hand, Einav Bublil's behaviour, unlike that of Shifra Korenfeld, is perceived as mere antics, as a kind of vulgar, embarrassing behaviour that is

---

42 For further information, see: http://www.Ynet.Co.Il/Articles/0,7340,L-3707536,00.Html.

43 Michael Mario Albrecht, *Fake Plastic Trees: Authenticity in Contemporary Popular Media Culture* (2009), http://books.google.co.il/books?id=L2Fqcgjy8-QC&pg=PA111&dq=fandom+authenticity&hl=iw&sa=X&ei=jb_JUeCwINHLtAbl_oHgAw&ved=0CE8Q6AEwBQ#v=onepage&q=fandom%20authenticity&f=false.

44 Uta Jaenicke, "The Issue of Human Existence as Represented in Dreaming: A New Daseinsanalytic Interpretation of the Meaning of Dreams," *International Forum of Psychoanalysis* 17 (2008): 51–5.

deemed eligible to walk the walk of shame.[45] When she decided to get married, Shifra Korenfeld was interested in getting romantically involved with a high-quality man. Still, the panel of judges presented a traditional approach according to which female Israeli celebs must have a man at their side. They are only worthy of publicity when they are in the framework of a heterosexual romantic relationship. It is also interesting that the panel of judges chose to present the celeb by her maiden name, with which she won public recognition in Israel. In many cultures, women who retain their maiden name are considered less community-spirited, less collegial, than women who change their names after marriage.[46] Thus, despite the fact that (American) law does not require a name change, in past years an increasing number of women have changed their names after marriage.[47] One of the obvious reasons for this is the desire to create a symbolic representation that runs parallel with their other lifestyle choices.[48] Simply put, married women today place great importance on their public nominative representative. Celebrities that walk the walk of shame are much less likely to enjoy such a public privilege.

Shifra Korenfeld and Einav Bublil's fan communities did not remain indifferent to the choice of their heroines as recipients of the Israel Celebs Awards, and they responded with talkbacks: "Shifra is Israel's quality sweetheart"; "Our darling Shifra, we are with you all the way!"; "Shifra, it isn't Yom Kippur, but can you forgive?"; "Shifra is worthy of every major cultural prize'; 'Shifra represents the best of charm and quality"; "Nobody beats Shifra! There's nothing bad to be said about her"; "Einav Bublil, I love you…you're the best"; "Einavi, you're a princess—you deserve it"; "Einav, I'm still in love with you to this very day"; "I'm obsessed by you…I'm in a bad way"; "In the entire world there is nobody better than Einav Bublil, even if we searched forever"; "Einav, we love you!"[49] It seems as though these fan communities completely ignored the criticism inherent in awarding the prizes and the judges' justifications for them and focused only on the emotions aroused in them by the objects of their adulation. Thus, similarly

---

45   Andrea Mayr, "Chopper from the Inside: Discourses of the 'Celebrity' Criminal Mark Brandon Read," *Language and Literature* 21 (2012): 260–73.

46   Claire E. Etaug, Judith S. Bridges, Myra Cummings-Hill and Joseph Cohen, "Names Can Never Hurt Me? The Effects of Surname Use on Perceptions of Married Women," *Psychology of Women Quarterly* 23 (1999): 819–23.

47   Claudia Goldin and Maria Shim, "Making a Name: Women's Names at Marriage and Beyond," *Journal of Economic Perspectives* 18 (2004): 143–60.

48   Laura Hamilton, Claudia Geist and Brian Powell, "Marital Name Change as a Window into Gender Attitudes," *Gender and Society* 25 (2011): 145–75.

49   For further information, see: http://www.ynet.co.il/articles/0,7340,L-3707536,00.html.

to fan communities in Canada, Israeli stardom also relies on the contrast of an imaginary relationship between ordinariness and extraordinariness.[50]

Within the themes characteristic of fan communities, text is coded into new patterns that provide points of departure through which fans are able to connect[51] among themselves as well as between themselves and their idols. Unlike other fan communities,[52] in the above discourse, Israeli fans are not really interested in active discussion; they prefer to focus on idolising local TV reality stars. This is more a declaration of love than a complex dialogue in which respondents employ broad metaphors.[53] In the present case, both those identifying with a representative of "high" culture and those supporting an example of "low" culture made simple, basic statements. This shows that fan communities make no distinction between high and low, and relate to both celebs in similar ways. This is how fan communities contribute to the postmodern blurring of boundaries between elitist and popular.

In 2012, ten scientists, theoreticians and social activists won the Israel Prize. Among the winners was the psychologist Professor Shlomo Benatin. Prof. Shlomo Benatin was chosen to receive the Israel Prize due to his scientific contribution to psychology in general and to cognitive psychology and neuropsychology in particular.[54] As a member of the intellectual elite, Prof. Shlomo Benatin is a well-known figure in his community. Like other members of intellectual elites who may exist as separate entities,[55] which promote intellectual discourse in rather closed circles, he is recognised as an authority in his own field, yet his celebrity image does not exist beyond the academic world. The significance of this is that unlike other cases, Israel Prize winners do not succeed in winning popular publicity that reflects the admiration of their work. The absence of such a mirror image is an inability to enter the charmed circle of celebrities.[56]

---

50 Nandy, "Fame and Nation: National Identity of Pop Star Justin Bieber," 13–21.
51 Rebecca W. Black, *Adolescents and Online Fan Fiction* (New York, NY: Peter Lang Publishing, Inc., 2008).
52 Ryan M. Milner, "'Fallout' Fans: Negotiations over Text Integrity in the Age of the Active Audience" (2008), http://www.academia.edu/1333272/Fallout_fans_Negotiations_over_text_integrity_in_the_age_of_the_active_audience.
53 Ingrid Piller, "Extended Metaphor in Automobile Fan Discourse," *Poetics Today* 20, no. 3 (1999): 483–98.
54 For further information, see: http://Cms.Education.Gov.Il/Educationcms/Units/Prasisrael/Mekableyprastashab/Shlomobenatin/Nimukim.htm.
55 Frederic Cople Jaher, *The Urban Establishment: Upper Strata in Boston, New York* (Illinois: University of Illinois Press, 1982).
56 Anna Fomichenko, "Oscar Wilde's Celebrity: Public Persona as a Character," in *The Performance of Celebrity*, ed. Amber A. Colvin (Oxford, UK: Inter-Disciplinary Press, 2013), 3–11.

In that same year, the Israel Celebs Award was bestowed upon seven celebrities, two men and five women. The lifetime achievement award for a special contribution to society and the state was awarded to Ms. Yonit Levi, a journalist and TV and radio personality who currently presents Channel 2's evening news broadcast. Yonit Levi was born in Jerusalem and grew up in an exclusive neighbourhood near the Hebrew University campus, where she attained a degree in English literature and history. Her career has led her to key positions in the Israeli media world, while her public face faithfully represents elitist society. On the other hand, she won local celebrity status due to her decision to cancel her honeymoon due to work obligations. Among the judges' reasons for their choice was:

> With consummate professionalism, and with the help of her stunning beauty, Ms. Levi succeeded in positioning herself as the most worthy woman in Israel. Furthermore, Ms. Levi took a small step for herself and a large step for the State of Israel when she married her beloved, Ido Rosenblum, and managed to deny the citizens of the state as much as a peek at this most important news event. In addition, Ms. Levi sacrificed her honeymoon with her new groom for the sake of a special news broadcast that covered the release of Gilad Shalit from the hands of Hamas. However, she did not entirely give up quality time with her husband, thus helping to increasing Israel's birth rate. For these reasons among others, Ms. Levi has been found worthy of receiving the lifetime achievement award on the 64th anniversary of the State of Israel.[57]

Here again one can observe the importance of marriage for celeb culture. The celebrity marriage may be seen as a cultural update of the power couple.[58] In fact, we can look at celebrities' relationships as larger-than-life archetypes of all relationships.[59] However, for women especially, marriage can be the proverbial double-edge sword. American culture, like its Israeli counterpart, pressures women into marriage so insistently that it can be viewed as an end in itself. Thus, celebrity marriages can be said to be both traditional (since they

---

57   For further information, see: http://www.Ynet.co.il/Articles/0,7340,L-4219169,00.Html.
58   Jonathan Goldman, *Modernism Is the Literature of Celebrity* (Austin, TX: The University of Texas Press, 2011).
59   Lawrence Cooper and Scott Baio, *Cult of Celebrity: What Our Fascination with the Stars Reveals about Us* (Guilford, CT: Morris Publishing Group, 2009).

include conservative social customs) and non-traditional.[60] The love between the bride and groom may be seen as evoking worship.[61]

Not surprisingly, Yonit Levi's fan community did not remain indifferent to her receiving the prize and responded with vehement talkbacks: "Nobody beats our ice princess, Yonit Levi!!!!"; "In her last photo Yonit Levi looks about 19 years old. She is amazing and an excellent newscaster"; "Yonit Levi is just gorgeous"; "Queen Yonit!!!!"; "One can only marvel at delightful Yonit Levi"; "Yonit is the end! She is just as lovely as she is intelligent. One could die for her…"; Yonit Levi is smart, pretty, charming," etc.[62]

But there was also an opposing camp that expressed its distaste for Yonit Levi: "Despite her good looks, Yonit Levi is a disgusting person"; "I don't understand why they make such a big fuss of that lemon"; "Yonit Levi is a terrible, unprofessional news presenter"; "Yonit Levi…[is] a spoiled child"; "I'm not crazy about Yonit Levi"; Do me a favour: Yonit Levi makes me sick," etc.[63] Thus, in opposition to expressions of adulation and appraisal of the physical and professional traits of the Israel Celebs Award for 2012, Yonit Levi appears to arouse negative criticism, that is just as powerful, regarding her qualities and abilities. This seems to be a binary contrast of two poles that generate a complete spectrum due to the tension between them—fans vs. opponents. Yonit, who has become a cultural hero, portrays in her media persona a talented ice princess who prefers to contribute a rational point of view on the public sphere wrapped in a particularly attractive outer shell.

5   Summary

This chapter began with the comparison between two celebrity communities: academics who represent high culture and belong to Israel's elite scientific, social and cultural community, and celebs who represent Israel's low culture as members of the reality show refugee community. From the results of the present chapter it appears that despite the diametrically opposed goals of the prizes, the general public perceives them both as honorary prizes. In other words, the Israel Prize represents the idea that the state is interested in paying

---

60   Jonathan Silverman, *Nine Choices: Johnny Cash and American Culture* (Massachusetts: University of Massachusetts Press, 2010).
61   Grahame Miles, *Science and Religious Experience: Are They Similar Forms of Knowledge?* (Portland, OR: Sussex Academic Press, 2007).
62   For further information, see: http://www.ynet.co.il/articles/0,7340,L-4219169,00.html.
63   For further information, see Ibid.

homage to its top scientists, social activists and artists. As is true elsewhere, the government awards the prize after certain judging and appraising mechanisms on the part of prominent academics have been put into motion, thus emphasising the greatness of the winners' achievements.[64] Clearly, such ceremonies reject any attempt at censure, ridicule or contempt. Similarly, Israeli fan community absolutely rejects the contemptuous tone of the Israel Celebs Awards (as opposed to the aims of those who bestow them) and ignores the public humiliation involved in openly declaring that the winners wallow in the celebrity swamp. The internet site that announces the prize seems mainly to arouse expressions of adulation or repugnance towards the winners, without referring to the cynical manner in which they were chosen.

This indicates that although celebrity culture constitutes an integral part of post-modern life, in the Israeli case, as presented above, the post-modern conditions which encourage a lack of valid absolute meaning over time are actually rejected. The results indicate that there is a desire to return to absolute values[65] and moral truth. In such cases, the characteristics of the social and cultural hierarchy are clear to everyone, and there is no doubt regarding the products and categories of "high" and "low."

Furthermore, celebrity worship, as well as the desire to be a celebrity, is often constructed as becoming part of an elite, the most desirable group and the community of the well-known.[66] Hence, fandom can be read as a performative politics of identity by which fans attempt to gain power and position themselves as close as possible to the elite. By expressing their love and admiration, they reinforce their commitment to the symbolic order. Moreover, since mass recognition is said to be concentrated on a symbolic elite of celebrities belonging to a very restricted population,[67] celebrity worship enables the fan community to "make peace" with the extremely symbolic dividing line between celebrities and so-called "ordinary" individuals.[68]

---

64 Alex Rosenberg, "Designing a Successor to the Patent as Second Best Solution to the Problem of Optimum Provision of Good," in *New Frontiers in the Philosophy of Intellectual Property*, ed. Annabelle Lever (Cambridge, UK: Cambridge University Press, 2012), 88–109.
65 David P. Marshall, *Celebrity and Power: Fame in Contemporary Culture* (Minneapolis, MN: University of Minnesota Press, 1997).
66 Jason Lee, *Celebrity, Pedophilia, and Ideology in American Culture* (Amherst, NY: Cambria Press, 2009).
67 Su Holmes and Sean Remond, "Introduction: Understanding Celebrity Culture," in *Framing Celebrity: New Directions in Celebrity Culture*, eds. Su Holmes and Sean Redmond (New York, NY: Routledge, 2006), 1–16.
68 David Holmes, *Communication Theory: Media, Technology and Society* (London: Sage, 2005).

Finally, the attempt to embarrass Israeli celebrities for their behaviour by creating a symbolic analogy between the Israel Prize and the Israel Celebs Awards seems to have been absolutely rejected by the fan community, which totally ignores the subversive nature of the prize and adheres only to the character of the celebrity who received it. This being so, it appears that in actual fact both the awarding of the Israel Prize and the Israel Celebs Awards on Independence Day reinforces the completeness of the fabric of Israeli society. In fact, rejecting the sarcastic tone of the Israel Celebs Awards and symbolically comparing them to the Israel Prize allows populations that are not numbered among intellectual elites to express their cultural preferences. The fans' total rejection of the sarcastic comparison between these prize-giving ceremonies celebrating the contribution of members of "high" society and those celebrating the contribution of members of the "low" cultural milieu actually helps preserve the above dichotomous distinction. Furthermore, even when in the sphere of celeb culture someone is perceived as a member of the "high-brow" intellectual elite, fan communities that generally support down-to-earth, authentic "low-brow" figures tend to gather around those cultural representatives. As such, celeb culture continues to develop as a system of signs organised in a structure having dichotomous contrasts that reflect the structuralist nature of society.

Bibliography

Adorno, T.W. *Minima Moralia*. London: Verso, 1974.

Albrecht, Michael Mario. *Fake Plastic Trees: Authenticity in Contemporary Popular Media Culture*. 2009. http://books.google.co.il/books?id=L2Fqcgjy8-QC&pg=PA111&dq=fandom+authenticity&hl=iw&sa=X&ei=jb_JUeCwINHLtAbl_oHgAw&ved=0CE8Q6AEwBQ#v=onepage&q=fandom%20authenticity&f=false.

Ashworth, John, Jaime C. Confer, Cari Goetz, and David Buss. "Expert Judgments and the Demand for Novels in Flanders." *Journal of Cultural Economics* 34 (2010): 197–218.

Baym, Nancy K. "The Emergence of Community in Computer-Mediated Communication." In *Cybersociety: Computer-Mediated Communication and Community*, edited by S. Jones, 138–63. Thousand Oaks, CA: Sage, 1995.

Baym, Nancy K. *Tune In, Log On: Soaps, Fandom, and Online Community*. Thousand Oaks, CA: Sage, 2000.

Benson, Fraser, and William Brown. "Media, Celebrities and Social Influence: Identification with Elvis Presley." *Mass Communication & Society* 5 (2002): 183–207.

Bielby, Denise D., Lee C. Harrington, and William T. Bielby. "Whose Stories Are They? Fans' Engagement with Soap Opera Narratives in Three Sites of Fan Activity." *Journal of Broadcasting and Electronic Media* 43 (1999): 35–51.

Bird, Cindy M. "Phenomenological Realities or Quinntown: Life in a Cyber Community." *Journal of American and Comparative Cultures* 25 (2002): 32–7.

Black, Rebecca W. *Adolescents and Online Fan Fiction*. New York, NY: Peter Lang Publishing, Inc., 2008.

Busse, Kristina, and Karen Hellekson, eds. *Fan Fiction and Fan Communities in the Age of the Internet: New Essays*. Jefferson, NC: McFarland Company, Inc., Publishers, 2006.

Cooper, Lawrence, and Scott Baio. *Cult of Celebrity: What Our Fascination with the Stars Reveals about Us*. Guilford, CT: Morris Publishing Group, 2009.

Darling-Wolf, Fabienne. "Virtually Multicultural: Trans-Asian Identity and Gender in an International Fan Community of a Japanese Star." *New Media Society* 6, no. 4 (2004): 507–28.

Eagleton, Terry. *Literacy Theory: An Introduction*. Oxford: Basil Blackwell, 1996.

Eco, Umberto, *The Open Work*. Cambridge, MA: Harvard University Press, 1989.

English, James F. *The Economy of Prestige: Prizes, Awards, and the Circulation of Cultural Value*. Harvard: Harvard University Press, 2005.

Etaug, Claire E., Judith S. Bridges, Myra Cummings-Hill, and Joseph Cohen. "Names Can Never Hurt Me? The Effects of Surname Use on Perceptions of Married Women." *Psychology of Women Quarterly* 23 (1999): 819–23.

Fiske, John. "The Cultural Economy of Fandom." In *The Adoring Audience: Fan Culture and Popular Media*, edited by L. Lewis, 30–49. London: Routledge, 1992.

Fitzgerald, Tanya, and Julia Savage, "Beyond Anonymity and the Everyday: Celebrity and the Capture of Educational Leadership." *Educational Review* 66, no. 1 (2014): 46–58.

Fomichenko, Anna. "Oscar Wilde's Celebrity: Public Persona as a Character." In *The Performance of Celebrity*, edited Amber A. Colvin, 3–11. Oxford, UK: Inter-Disciplinary Press, 2013.

Frow, John. *Cultural Studies and Cultural Value*. Oxford: Clarendon Press, 1995.

Gans, Herbert. *Popular Culture and High Culture: An Analysis and Evaluation of Taste*. New York: Basic Books, 1999.

Goldin, Claudia, and Maria Shim. "Making A Name: Women's Names at Marriage and Beyond." *Journal of Economic Perspectives* 18 (2004): 143–60.

Goldman, Jonathan. *Modernism Is the Literature of Celebrity*. Austin, TX: The University of Texas Press, 2011.

Grossberg, Lawrence. "Is There a Fan in the House?: The Affective Sensibility of Fandom." In *The Adoring Audience: Fan Culture and Popular Media*, edited by L. Lewis, 50–68. London: Routledge, 1992.

Gurevitz, David, and Dan Arav. *Encyclopedia of Ideas*. Tel Aviv: Babel and Yedioth Media Group, 2012. [Hebrew].

Hamilton, Laura, Claudia Geist, and Brian Powell. "Marital Name Change as a Window into Gender Attitudes." *Gender and Society* 25 (2011): 145–75.

Harrington, Carine Lee, and Denise D. Bielby. *Soap Fans: Pursuing Pleasure and Making Meaning in Everyday Life*. Philadelphia: Temple University Press, 1995.

Heinich, Nathalie. "The Sociology of Vocational Prizes: Recognition as Esteem." *Theory Culture Society* 26 (2009): 85–107.

Hills, Matt. *Fan Cultures*. London: Routledge, 2002.

Holmes, David. *Communication Theory: Media, Technology and Society*. London: Sage, 2005.

Holmes, Su, and Sean Remond. "Introduction: Understanding Celebrity Culture." In *Framing Celebrity: New Directions in Celebrity Culture*, edited by Su Holmes, and Sean Redmond, 1–16. New York, NY: Routledge, 2006.

Jaenicke, Uta. "The Issue of Human Existence as Represented in Dreaming: A New Daseinsanalytic Interpretation of the Meaning of Dreams." *International Forum of Psychoanalysis* 17 (2008): 51–5.

Jaher, Frederic Cople. *The Urban Establishment: Upper Strata in Boston, New York*. Illinois: University of Illinois Press, 1982.

Jenkins, Henry. *Textual Poachers: Television Fans and Participatory Culture*. New York: Routledge, 1992.

Lee, Jason. *Celebrity, Pedophilia, and Ideology in American Culture*. Amherst, NY: Cambria Press, 2009.

Marshall, David P. *Celebrity and Power: Fame in Contemporary Culture*. Minneapolis, MN: University of Minnesota Press, 1997.

Mayer, Sandra. "En*Nobel*ing Literary Celebrity: Authorial Self-Fashioning in the Nobel Lectures of Elfriede Jelinek and Harold Pinter." In *The Performance of Celebrity*, edited by Amber A. Colvin, 67–80. Oxford, UK: Inter-Disciplinary Press, 2013.

Mayr, Andrea. "Chopper: From the Inside: Discourses of the "Celebrity" Criminal Mark Brandon Read." *Language and Literature* 21 (2012): 260–73.

Miles, Grahame. *Science and Religious Experience: Are They Similar Forms of Knowledge?* Portland, OR: Sussex Academic Press, 2007.

Milner, Ryan M. "'Fallout' Fans: Negotiations over Text Integrity in the Age of the Active Audience." 2008. http://www.academia.edu/1333272/Fallout_fans_Negotiations_over_text_integrity_in_the_age_of_the_active_audience.

Moran, Joe. *Star Authors: Literary Celebrity in America*. London: Pluto Press, 2000.

Morrill, Calvin, and William Bailey. "The Reciprocal Power Identities and Social Style: A Note on a Specimen Deviant Youth Group." In *Postmodern Political Communication: The Fringe Challenges the Center*, edited by Andrew King, 32–57. Westport, CT: Praeger Publishers, 1992.

Moshe, Mira. "The 'Israel Celebs Awards': The Walk of Shame on the Way to Fame." In *The Walk of Shame*, edited by Mira Moshe, and Nicoleta Corbu, 77–92. New York, NY: Nova Science Publishers, 2013.

Moshe, Mira, and Nicoleta Corbu, eds. *The Walk of Shame*. New York, NY: Nova Science Publishers, 2013.

Nandy, Samita. "Fame and Nation: National Identity of Pop Star Justin Bieber." In *The Performance of Celebrity*, edited by Amber A. Colvin, 13–21. Oxford, UK: Inter-Disciplinary Press, 2013.

Peterson, Richard A. "Understanding Audience Segmentation: From Elite and Mass to Omnivore and Univore/" *Poetics* 21 (1992): 243–58.

Piller, Ingrid. "Extended Metaphor in Automobile Fan Discourse." *Poetics Today* 20, no. 3 (1999): 483–98.

Radford, Scott K., and Peter H. Bloch. "Grief, Commiseration and Consumption Following the Death of a Celebrity." *Journal of Consumer Culture* 12, no. 2 (2012): 137–55.

Rajagopalan, Sudha. "Shahrukh Khan as Media Text: Celebrity, Identity and Emotive Engagement in a Russian Online Community." *Celebrity Studies* 2, no. 3 (2011): 263–76.

Rosenberg, Alex. "Designing a Successor to the Patent as Second Best Solution to the Problem of Optimum Provision of Good." In *New Frontiers in the Philosophy of Intellectual Property*, edited by Annabelle Lever, 88–109. Cambridge, UK: Cambridge University Press, 2012.

Sandstrom, Kent L., Daniel D. Martin, and Gary Alan Fine. *Symbols, Selves, and Social Reality*. New York: Oxford University Press, 2006.

Silverman, Jonathan. *Nine Choices: Johnny Cash and American Culture*. Massachusetts: University of Massachusetts Press, 2010.

Soukup, Charles. "Hitching a Ride on a Star: Celebrity, Fandom, and Identification on the World Wide Web." *Southern Communication Journal* 71, no. 4 (2006): 319–37.

Ter Bogt, Tom F.M., Juul Mulder, A.W. Quinten Raaijmakers, and Saoirse Nic Gabhainn, "Moved by Music: A Typology of Music Listeners." *Psychology of Music* 39 (2011) 147–63.

Whittenberger-Keith, Kari. "Understanding Fandom Rhetorically: The Case of 'Beauty and the Beast.'" In *Postmodern Political Communication: The Fringe Challenges the Center*, edited by Andrew King, 131–52. Santa Barbara, CA: Praeger Publishers, 1992.

Williams, Zachery R. *In Search of the Talented Tenth: Howard University Public Intellectuals and the Dilemmas of Race, 1926–1970*. Colombia, MI: University of Missouri Press, 2009.

York, Lorraine Mary. *Literary Celebrity in Canada*. Toronto: University of Toronto Press, 2007.

Index

Accessibility   5, 40, 42, 49, 64, 98, 99, 103–104, 105, 110, 111, 114
Anderson, Benedict   35
Anglo-Irish Treaty   13, 16
Authenticity   3, 5, 21, 34–35, 38–39, 42, 44, 45–48, 49–51, 70, 104, 127

Bakhtin, Mikhail   78, 88
Benatin, Shlomo   129
Bieber, Justin   3, 14, 22, 34–53
Bourdieu, Pierre   58, 127
Bowie, David   4, 77, 81, 85–91
Bublil, Einav   126–128

Canada   34–53, 129
Celebrity
    As a brand   3, 11, 13, 22, 25–28, 34, 39, 48–51, 54, 57
    Definition   13, 35, 39, 96, 102
    Expiration of   4, 77–78, 83, 90, 91
    "extraordinary"   2, 3, 34, 35, 44, 51, 93, 98, 101, 106, 107, 109
    As a hero   6, 12–14, 28, 34–38, 41, 46–48, 86, 110, 131
    Literary   54–74, 77–92
    Local   93–118
    Martyrdom   11–12, 23, 25, 29, 47
    Notoriety   6, 13, 59, 81
    Online   3, 14, 34–35, 39–43, 51–52, 106
    "ordinary"   5, 35, 44, 51, 93, 99–101, 102, 104, 105, 132
    Sport   93–118
Collins, Michael   11–33
Culture
    high/low   119–136

death portrait   12, 24
"D-List"   101
Douglas, Lord Alfred   84–85
Dyer, Richard   39, 41

Fame monstrosity   90
Fan(s) studies   4, 114

fin de siècle   82, 86, 90
Fry, Stephen   85, 86

Gender   56, 93, 94, 95, 100, 112, 113

Hortons, Tim   22, 48–51

Iconicity   24
Industrialisation   35
Irish, the   11–33
Israel
    Israel Celebs Awards   119–136
    Israel Prize   119–136

Jelinek, Elfriede   4, 54–57, 59–61, 68–70

Korenfeld, Shifra   126–128

Lavery, Sir John   12, 24–25
Levi, Yonit   130–131
littérature engagée   65

Nationalism   11–33, 34–53
Neeson, Liam   27
Nobel Prize   54–74

Pinter, Harold   4, 54, 55–56, 59–60, 62, 65–68, 70
Pope Francis   1–2

Rojek, Chris   1, 36
Roller Derby   93–118

Sinn Fein   12
Sports   93–118
Sydney   93–118
Skaters   93–118

Touch   5, 21, 93, 99, 107–108
Turner, Graeme   97

Wilde, Oscar   56, 57, 77–92, 103

Printed in the United States
By Bookmasters